1900

Volume I 1910

This Fabulous Century

Sixty Years of American Life

1900 1910

Volume I

By the Editors of TIME-LIFE BOOKS

Time-Life Books, New York

TIME-LIFE BOOKS

EDITOR
Maitland A. Edey

EXECUTIVE EDITOR
Jerry Korn

TEXT DIRECTOR   ART DIRECTOR
Martin Mann   Sheldon Cotler

CHIEF OF RESEARCH
Beatrice T. Dobie

PICTURE EDITOR
Robert G. Mason

Assistant Text Directors:
Harold C. Field, Ogden Tanner
Assistant Art Director: Arnold C. Holeywell
Assistant Chief of Research: Martha T. Goolrick

PUBLISHER
Rhett Austell

Associate Publisher: Walter C. Rohrer
Assistant Publisher: Carter Smith
General Manager: Joseph C. Hazen Jr.
Business Manager: John D. McSweeney
Production Manager: Louis Bronzo
Sales Director: Joan D. Manley
Promotion Director: Beatrice K. Tolleris
Managing Director, International:
John A. Millington

THIS FABULOUS CENTURY

SERIES EDITOR: Ezra Bowen
Editorial Staff for *Volume I, 1900-1910*
Picture Editor: Mary Y. Steinbauer
Designer: John R. Martinez
Staff Writers: George Constable,
Anne Horan, Gerald Simons, Bryce S. Walker
Researchers: Alice Baker, Nancy Cabasin,
Terry Drucker, Helen Greenway, Helen Lapham,
Victoria Winterer, Linda Wolfe
Art Assistant: Anne B. Landry

EDITORIAL PRODUCTION
Color Director: Robert L. Young
Assistant: James J. Cox
Copy Staff: Marian Gordon Goldman,
Susan B. Galloway, Florence Keith
Picture Department: Dolores A. Littles,
Barbara S. Simon
Traffic: Arthur A. Goldberger
Studio: Herbert Quarmby

The following individuals and departments of Time Inc. gave valuable aid in the preparation of this book: Editorial Production, Robert W. Boyd Jr; Editorial Reference, Peter Draz; Picture Collection, Doris O'Neil; Photographic Laboratory, George Karas; TIME-LIFE News Service, Richard M. Clurman; Correspondents Jane Beatty (Philadelphia); Robert Buyer (Buffalo); Patricia Chandler (New Orleans); Don Davies (Madison); Jane Estes (Seattle); Martha Green (San Francisco); Julie Greenwalt (Detroit); Blanche Hardin (Denver); Sandra Hinson (Orlando); Lucille Larkin (Washington, D.C.); Frank Leeming Jr. (St. Louis); Holland McCombs (Dallas); Reg Murphy (Atlanta); Richard Rawe (Cincinnati); Jane Rieker (Miami); Gayle Rosenberg (Los Angeles); Sherley Uhl (Pittsburgh); Rod Van Every (Milwaukee); Richard Wootten (Cleveland); Sue Wymelenberg (Boston).

Contents

Introduction

At the outgoing of the old and the incoming of the new century you begin the last session of the Fifty-sixth Congress with evidences on every hand of individual and national prosperity and with proof of the growing strength and increasing power for good of Republican institutions.

PRESIDENT WILLIAM McKINLEY TO THE CONGRESS, DECEMBER 3, 1900

When President McKinley proudly addressed the Congress at the turn of the century, America was a country very different from the colossus it was to become. The statistics of the period (imperfect though they were in those non-computerized times) illustrate the contrast dramatically. In 1900 there were only 45 states—despite the optimistic 48-star flag on page 19. The total U.S. population was 76,094,000—barely two fifths what it would be six decades later. The average American worker earned 22¢ an hour. Automobiles were selling for about $1,550 each; and the truck and bus were still to be invented. In any case, fewer than 150 miles of paved highway existed in the whole United States.

Keeping up with the Joneses had not yet become a national religion. Only about 18 people in every 1,000 owned a telephone, and there was still no such thing as a radio or an electric ice box or most of the other symbols of modern domestic consumership. People had other, more fundamental things to worry about. Diphtheria, typhoid and malaria were among the leading causes of death. A cold might easily develop into pneumonia, and more often than not, pneumonia was fatal.

The most crowded occupation in the United States in 1900 was agriculture, for nearly 11 million people were farmers. But times were changing. Factory employment was already over six million and climbing fast. Nearly half a million immigrants poured into the country in 1900; within five years the annual total would be over a million. These newcomers were bringing change with them, and by their ways and their sheer numbers, too, they would help to cause change.

But in 1900, most of the changes had not yet taken hold. Life across the predominantly rural countryside was still relatively simple and, as President McKinley noted in his Congressional message, quite good. For almost two full generations there had been no major wars. This, too, seemed quite proper. The business of America was peace—peace and prosperity. And it was a fact that in this simple time even the U.S. Government was prosperous: in 1900 the Treasury showed a surplus of $46,380,000 in income over expenditures. This happy circumstance would occur again from time to time until 1960 *(page 9)* when President Dwight D. Eisenhower proudly balanced the U.S. national budget for the last time—while standing in a hole of gross debt so deep that the achievement was barely visible.

Population

	1900	1960
TOTAL UNITED STATES	76,094,000	179,323,000
URBAN (2500 or more)	30,160,000	113,056,000
Per cent	40%	63%
RURAL	45,835,000	66,267,000
Per cent	60%	37%
Native born white	56,595,000	149,544,000
Foreign born white	10,214,000	9,294,000
Negro	8,834,000	18,849,000
American Indian	237,000	547,000
Oriental	114,000	709,000

STATES BY POPULATION

Rank		1900	1960	Rank
1	New York	7,268,894	16,782,304	1
2	Pennsylvania	6,302,115	11,319,366	3
3	Illinois	4,821,550	10,081,158	4
4	Ohio	4,157,545	9,706,397	5
5	Missouri	3,106,665	4,319,813	13
6	Texas	3,048,710	9,579,677	6
7	Massachusetts	2,805,346	5,148,578	9
8	Indiana	2,516,462	4,662,498	11
9	Michigan	2,420,982	7,823,194	7
10	Iowa	2,231,853	2,757,537	24
11	Georgia	2,216,331	3,943,116	16
12	Kentucky	2,147,174	3,038,156	22
13	Wisconsin	2,069,042	3,951,777	15
14	Tennessee	2,020,616	3,567,089	17
15	North Carolina	1,893,810	4,556,155	12
16	New Jersey	1,883,669	6,066,782	8
17	Virginia	1,854,184	3,966,949	14
18	Alabama	1,828,697	3,266,740	19
19	Minnesota	1,751,394	3,413,864	18
20	Mississippi	1,551,270	2,178,141	29
21	California	1,485,053	15,717,204	2
22	Kansas	1,470,495	2,178,611	28
23	Louisiana	1,381,625	3,257,022	20
24	South Carolina	1,340,316	2,382,594	26
25	Arkansas	1,311,564	1,786,272	31
26	Maryland	1,188,044	3,100,689	21
27	Nebraska	1,066,300	1,411,330	34
28	West Virginia	958,800	1,860,421	30
29	Connecticut	908,420	2,535,234	25
30	Maine	694,466	969,265	36

STATES BY POPULATION (continued)

Rank		1900	1960	Rank
31	Colorado	539,700	1,753,947	33
32	Florida	528,542	4,951,560	10
33	Washington	518,103	2,853,214	23
34	Rhode Island	428,556	859,488	39
35	Oregon	413,536	1,768,687	32
36	New Hampshire	411,588	606,921	46
37	South Dakota	401,570	680,514	41
38	*Oklahoma Terr.	398,331		
39	*Indian Terr.	392,060	2,328,284	27
40	Vermont	343,641	389,881	48
41	North Dakota	319,146	632,446	45
42	Dist. of Columbia	278,718	763,956	40
43	Utah	276,749	890,627	38
44	Montana	243,329	674,767	42
45	**New Mexico Terr.	195,310	951,023	37
46	Delaware	184,735	446,292	47
47	Idaho	161,772	667,191	43
48	**Hawaii Terr.	154,001	632,772	44
49	**Arizona Terr.	122,931	1,302,161	35
50	Wyoming	92,531	330,066	49
51	**Alaska Terr.	63,592	226,167	51
52	Nevada	42,335	285,278	50

*Joined to become Oklahoma state 1907   **Became state after 1910

Immigration

	1900	1960
TOTAL ALL NATIONS	448,572	265,398
EUROPE		
Austria-Hungary	114,847	*
Italy	100,135	14,933
Russia and Baltic States	90,787	4,228
Ireland (Northern & Eire)	35,730	8,967
Scandinavia	31,151	6,379
Germany	18,507	31,768
Great Britain	12,509	23,363
Romania	6,459	993
Portugal	4,234	6,968
Greece	3,771	3,797

*Includes part or all of Austria, Hungary, Czechoslovakia, Poland

ASIA		
Japan	12,635	5,471
Turkey	3,962	674
China	1,247	3,681

Immigration *(continued)*

	1900	1960
AMERICAS		
West Indies and Miquelon	4,656	14,052
Canada	396	30,990
Mexico	237	32,684
South America	124	13,048
Central America	42	6,661
AFRICA	30	2,526
AUSTRALIA AND NEW ZEALAND	214	912

Education

	1900	1960
ELEMENTARY AND SECONDARY SCHOOLS		
Enrollment	16,855,000	41,778,000
High school graduates	95,000	1,864,000
Total public school faculty	423,000	1,387,000
Average salary in		
public school	$325	$5,174
Cost per pupil	$17	$472
HIGHER EDUCATION		
Enrollment	238,000	3,216,000
Undergraduate	232,000	2,874,000
Graduate school	6,000	342,000
Faculty	23,868	380,554
ILLITERACY PER CENT	10.7%	2.4%

Family Living

	1900	1960
Average size of family	4.7 persons	3.7 persons
Total families	16,188,000	45,062,000
Total divorces	56,000	393,000

Health

	1900	1960
AVERAGE LIFE EXPECTANCY	47.3 years	69.7 years
Male life expectancy	46.3 years	66.6 years
Female life expectancy	48.3 years	73.1 years
White life expectancy	47.6 years	70.6 years
Non-white life expectancy	33.0 years	63.6 years
Birth rate per 1,000	32.3	23.7
Death rate per 1,000	17.2	9.5
Death rate per 1,000 under 1 year	162.4	26.1
CAUSES OF DEATH PER 100,000		
Heart-Artery-Kidney diseases	345.2	521.8
Influenza and pneumonia	202.2	37.3
Tuberculosis	194.4	6.1
Gastro-intestinal diseases	142.7	4.4
Cancer	64.0	149.2
Diphtheria	40.3	less than 0.1
Typhoid and paratyphoid	31.3	less than 0.1
Malaria	19.5	less than 0.1
Measles	13.3	0.2
Whooping cough	12.2	0.1
Suicide	10.2	10.6
Appendicitis	6.7	1.0
Childbirth	5.9	0.9
Total motor vehicle deaths	under 100	38,137
Total executions	155	56
Total lynchings	115	none recorded

Labor

	1900	1960
TOTAL WORKING FORCE	29,030,000	70,612,000
Men working	23,711,000	47,025,000
Women working	5,319,000	23,587,000
Per cent unemployed	5%	5.6%
EMPLOYMENT BY MAJOR INDUSTRY		
Agriculture	10,710,000	4,256,000
Manufacturing	6,340,000	17,513,000
Service	3,210,000	5,470,000
Trade, finance and real estate	2,760,000	14,487,000
Transportation and other utilities	2,100,000	4,458,000
Construction	1,660,000	3,816,000
Mining	760,000	654,000
Forestry and fisheries	210,000	93,000

LABOR (continued)

SAMPLE OCCUPATIONS	1900	1960
Dressmakers (not factory)	413,000	119,000
Blacksmiths, forgemen and hammermen	220,000	32,000
Barbers and beauticians	133,000	480,000
Physicians	131,000	229,000
Bartenders	89,000	172,000
Milliners	75,000	4,000
Electricians	51,000	337,000
Telephone operators	19,000	357,000
Professional nurses (inc. students)	12,000	640,000
Newsboys	7,000	190,000
AVERAGE WAGE		
Per week	$12.74	$89.72
Per hour	$ 0.22	$ 2.26
AVERAGE WORK WEEK (in hours)	59.0	39.7

Transportation

RAILROADS	1900	1960
Passenger miles	16,038,000,000	21,284,000,000
Freight ton miles	141,597,000,000	575,360,000,000
No. of companies	1,224	407
Steam locomotives	37,463	374
Electric locomotives	200	498
Diesel locomotives	none	30,240
SHIPS		
Total commercial ships	23,333	43,088
Steam tonnage	2,658,000	23,553,000
Sail tonnage	1,885,000	23,000
AUTOMOBILES		
Total registered cars	8,000	61,682,000
Total registered trucks and buses	none	12,213,000
Maximum record speed	65.79 mph	394.1 mph
Total miles of paved roads	under 150	3,546,000
TROLLEY CARS	1902	1960
Total miles of track	22,577	2,196
Vehicle miles	1,144,000,000	100,700,000

Business

	1900	1960
GROSS NATIONAL PRODUCT	$16,800,000,000*	$502,600,000,000
Goods	$8,420,000,000	$257,100,000,000
Services	$4,440,000,000	$188,800,000,000
Other	$3,890,000,000	$56,700,000,000
IMPORTS	$1,179,000,000	$14,654,000,000
EXPORTS	$1,686,000,000	$20,550,000,000

*average over 5 year period 1897-1901

BUSINESS (continued)

TOP COMPANIES AND ASSETS	1909*	1960
United States Steel Corp.	$1,804,000,000	$4,781,000,000
Standard Oil Co., New Jersey	800,000,000	10,090,000,000
American Tobacco Co.	286,000,000	851,000,000
Int'l Mercantile Marine Co. now U.S. Lines Co.	192,000,000	40,000,000
Amalgamated Copper Co. now Anaconda Copper Co.	170,000,000	1,086,000,000
Int'l Harvester Co.	166,000,000	1,457,000,000
Central Leather Co.	138,000,000	dissolved
Pullman Co.	131,000,000	34,000,000
Armour & Co.	125,000,000	256,000,000
American Sugar Co.	124,000,000	197,000,000

*1900 figure not available

Communication

POST OFFICE	1900	1960
Pieces of matter handled	7,130,000,000	63,675,000,000
PRINTING		
New books published	4,490	12,069
Total daily newspapers	2,226	1,763
Circulation of daily newspapers	15,102,000	58,882,000
TELEPHONE AND TELEGRAPH		
Telephones per 1,000	17.6	408.1
Telegraph messages sent per 1,000	217.2	755.6

Government

	1900	1960
GROSS DEBT	$1,263,417,000	$286,471,000,000
TOTAL RECEIPTS	$567,241,000	$77,763,000,000
Internal revenue	$295,328,000	$73,291,000,000
Customs revenue	$233,165,000	$1,105,000,000
Miscellaneous	$38,748,000	$4,062,000,000
TOTAL EXPENDITURES	$520,861,000	$76,539,000,000
SURPLUS	$46,380,000	$1,224,000,000
TOTAL CIVILIAN EMPLOYEES	239,476*	2,430,000
SALARIES		
Member of Congress	$5,000	$22,500
Cabinet member	$8,000	$25,000
Vice President	$8,000	$35,000
President	$50,000	$100,000

*1901 (1900 figure not available)

Daytona Beach, Florida, about 1904.

America
1900·1910

13

New York City, after 1900.

Company outing, Waukesha Beach, Wisconsin, 1908.

Delivering ice, Cleveland, around 1910.

Fourth of July, Nome, Alaska, 1901.

Lunchtime, Minnesota farm, about 1900.

23   *The Erie Canal, Durhamville, New York, about 1905.*

Cotton-marketing day, Marietta, Georgia, 1905.

The finish of a transcontinental auto tour, 1904.

READING THE WILL

THE INHERITANCE OF THE XXᵀᴴ CENTURY

A feckless youth in sporty attire, the 20th Century whistles nonchalantly as he scans the mixed legacy of problems and assets bequeathed to him by the Old Century.

The Cocksure Era

The will to grow was everywhere written large, and to grow at no matter what or whose expense.

HENRY JAMES

It was a splendid time, a wonderful country. Most Americans felt that way as they welcomed the 20th Century, and many of them said so, with great animation and grandiose references to Peace, Prosperity and Progress.

From Senator Chauncey Depew of New York: "There is not a man here who does not feel 400 per cent bigger in 1900 than he did in 1896, bigger intellectually, bigger hopefully, bigger patriotically."

Depew's colleague, Mark Hanna of Ohio: "Furnaces are glowing, spindles are singing their song. Happiness comes to us all with prosperity."

The Reverend Newell Dwight Hillis of Brooklyn: "Laws are becoming more just, rulers humane; music is becoming sweeter and books wiser."

These statements set the mood for the first decade of the new century and won for the period several titles —the Age of Optimism, the Age of Confidence, the Age of Innocence. But another tag might have seemed more appropriate to an objective visitor from abroad: the Cocksure Era. For this was a time when Americans were optimistic and self-confident to an extreme; they did not merely hope for the best, they fully expected it. A welter of practical and moral problems—child labor, teeming slums, widespread offenses by corrupt politicians and ruthless corporations—could not shake the faith of Americans in the inevitability of their progress as individuals and as a nation. Most people automatically assumed that all problems would be solved in the normal course of events; meanwhile, the important thing was for a man to get ahead, to earn maximum returns from bountiful opportunities.

There was ample reason for high hopes and general satisfaction. The housewife found the stores well stocked and prices low: she could buy eggs for 12 cents a dozen, sirloin steak for 24 cents a pound, a turkey dinner for 20 cents. The farmer was doing well after some hard times in the '90s. For the businessman, taxes were minimal and trade was brisk; indeed, conditions were almost good enough to justify the Boston *Herald*'s verdict, "If one could not have made money this past year, his case is hopeless." Everyone was fascinated by the many useful devices coming to the fore: the telephone, the typewriter and the sewing machine, the self-binding harvester and even the automobile (fully 8,000 of these vehicles were registered by 1900). But to the thoughtful citizen, the surest portents of a brilliant future were the astonishing achievements of the recent American past.

In the 19th Century, American energy and individualism had written a national epic without historic parallel. A thin fringe of Eastern states with five million inhabitants had swelled into a continent-wide nation with a population of 76 million. In the 35 years since the Civil War, a predominantly agrarian country had vaulted from fourth place to first among the world's industrial powers; a loose collection of very different regions, permissively administered by the laissez-faire government, had been woven into a fairly homogeneous and interdependent unit by expanding railroad networks, lengthening newspaper chains and burgeoning techniques of mass production and nationwide marketing. And in just the past few years, the United States had fought and won an exhilarating war with Spain, emerging as a major military power with possessions and protectorates that sprawled from the Caribbean to the China Seas. The facts and figures—a veritable torrent of information on rich resources and soaring growth rates—promised that progress would continue at an accelerating speed.

Though no single fact could sum up America's past and present, the one that came closest was a casual item, appearing in the Census Bureau report for 1900, that brought brief fame to the small town of Columbus, Indiana. According to the report, the geographic center of population was now located near Columbus—a move of about 475 miles west since 1800. Implicit in the item were vast and ever-shifting patterns of migration: the arrival and dispersal of 19 million immigrants; the conquest of the western frontier; the rise of big cities where once had stood forests and prairies; the rise and decline of innumerable small towns—and, no less significant, the survival of countless towns and villages virtually unchanged in size and character, ideals and biases. In progressing from the good old days to complex modern times, America was changing faster than its people knew, but it was also remaining much the same.

Clearly each community, whether rural or urban, was a special case, subject to a unique combination of forces. Old boom towns such as Creede, Colorado, petered out along with their payloads, while a corona of new towns in Minnesota attested to the discovery of the Mesabi iron-ore range. The commercial success of furniture factories in Grand Rapids, Michigan, cut into the business

---

God has marked the American people as His chosen nation to finally lead in the regeneration of the world. This is the divine mission of America, and it holds for us all the profit, all the glory, all the happiness possible to man. We are trustees of the world's progress, guardians of its righteous peace.

SENATOR ALBERT J. BEVERIDGE OF INDIANA

---

of country cabinetmakers as far east as Litchfield, Connecticut; the displaced rural artisans drifted into the cities to seek new work. But the most far-reaching influence on the pattern of settlement was the railroads.

For countless communities, the route of a railroad made the difference between growth and decay. Along the 193,368 miles of track that crisscrossed America in 1900, hundreds of hamlets survived or were jerry-built in the middle of nowhere, because they were needed to service the panting locomotives, which had to take on water every 40 miles or so. These forlorn way stations gave birth to some particularly graphic American slang: "tank town," "whistle stop," "jerkwater." On the other hand, many thriving inland ports, such as Little Falls on the Erie Canal and Paducah on the Ohio River, saw their dreams of greatness crushed, and were reduced to provincial towns, as manufacturers shifted their shipments from barge and steamboat to the faster rail freights. Even celebrated ports on the Mississippi were affected; Cairo and Hannibal and other towns suffered population losses traceable in large degree to the rise of St. Louis as a major railroad center. The decline of the Mississippi traffic was sudden and steep. The lifetime of one former river-pilot, Mark Twain, embraced both the heyday and the twilight of the palatial sternwheeler. "A strangely short life," said the author sadly, "for so magnificent a creature."

The statistics told an ominous story to rural America. While 60 per cent of the U.S. population in 1900 lived on farms or in communities with less than 2,500 inhabitants, that percentage represented a nationwide shrinkage over the previous three decades. Rural New England had long since lost much of its population to the cities and to the Midwest; in turn, the rural Midwest had begun losing population to the cities and to the West as early as the 1870s. A survey of 6,291 small towns in five Midwestern states for the decade ending in 1890 revealed that fully 3,144 communities had recorded appreciable losses in population. By 1908, the continuing decline of the small town was causing such concern that President Theodore Roosevelt set up a commission to make an investigation.

Nevertheless, magazine articles announcing "The Doom of the Small Town" proved premature. It was true that many young men, attracted by the opportunities and excitement of the cities, departed on that classic journey by day coach to make a name or a fortune on the urban frontier; many rural towns, stripped of their most promising people, became, as an unfriendly observer put it, "fished-out ponds populated chiefly by bullheads and suckers." But at the same time many country towns attained a kind of stability and fulfilled useful purposes even in eclipse. Resolutely conservative in all things, they served as restraints on the pace of progress, as strongholds of the stern old-time religion, as custodians of homely virtues and ideals taught generations by McGuffey's *Readers*, as islands of security and leisure amid the hustle and hazards of modern times. In rural America God was surely in His heaven and all was right with the world.

Nostalgia for the country hometown staked a permanent claim on the American imagination. The close-knit relationships of rural life—that sense of belonging which author Zona Gale glorified under the name of "Togetherness"—cast a spell on even those who had never lived in a small town. Five former country boys, yearning for lost Togetherness in Chicago, manufactured an urban substitute in 1905; they founded the Rotary Club, whose membership grew in coldly impersonal cities from coast to coast. Many a man made a sentimental journey to his rural hometown, there to savor again its changeless peace and order, the kindness and informality of its people.

Despite the appeal of country towns, the cities grew ever more populous. They received a vastly disproportionate share of the 8.8 million immigrants who arrived in America during the decade. The newcomers, most of them poor Italians and Russians and Poles and Jews, found plenty of work in the mining towns of Pennsylvania and West Virginia, in the sweatshops of New York and Chicago, in the mills and plants of Pitts-

---

The rights and interests of the laboring man will be protected and cared for—not by labor agitators, but by the Christian men to whom God in His infinite wisdom has given the control of the property interests of the country.

GEORGE F. BAER, PRESIDENT, PHILADELPHIA & READING RAILWAY

---

burgh, St. Louis and Cincinnati. Here the newcomers also found plenty of countrymen; immigration in the 19th Century had been so heavy that one third of the people in the United States in 1900 were foreign born or were the children of foreign born.

The cities bulged upward in skyscrapers and tall apartment houses, and outward in jumbles of slums and mansions, grimy factories and cheap-Jack entertainment centers. The population of three cities—New York, Chicago and Philadelphia—had topped the million mark by 1900. Secondary cities—Cleveland, St. Louis and Los Angeles—were much smaller but growing fast.

Growth rates could be used to form a general notion of the city's future, but they were inaccurate indicators. Nevertheless, at the turn of the century, when civic pride and boisterous optimism inspired a spate of fu-

NEW YORK CITY AS IT WILL BE IN 1999

COPYRIGHT 1900 BY THE PRESS PUB CO

SUPPLEMENT TO THE N.Y. WORLD DEC 30, 1900

PICTORIAL FORECAST OF THE CITY AS APPROVED BY ANDREW H. GREEN, H.H. VREELAND, and JOHN B. MC DONALD.

TOPOGRAPHICAL MAP OF NEW YORK A CENTURY HENCE — IN 1999

A futuristic drawing done in 1900 portrays the New York City of 1999 crammed with skyscrapers, overflown by airships and served by a network of bridges.

turistic articles and illustrations (left), local experts applied the figures with great self-confidence. Various New Yorkers, attempting to calculate the population of their metropolis in the year 1999, arrived by way of the same statistics at predictions ranging anywhere from eight to 45 million. One oracle, noting that automobiles were shorter than horse-drawn vehicles and that auto engines were cleaner than horses, reached the wild conclusion that the cities of tomorrow would have immaculate streets and no traffic jams.

No one, not even the most imaginative prophet, could have predicted in 1900 what was about to happen to a sunbaked Oklahoma hamlet known locally as Tulsey town. Tulsey town itself might well have looked to the past rather than the future. Long an Indian meeting place, it was a small cowtown in 1900; its population was only 1,340, and the town consisted of a single dirt street lined with ramshackle buildings. According to the local press, freight-car business for the first week of 1900 was far from encouraging: "Receipts: one car bran; shipments: two cars hogs, one car sand, one car mules." The big story of the day was half business, half social event: Chief Frank Corndropper was soon to give his daughter Mary in marriage and to receive in return the groom's gift of several hundred ponies.

But 18 months later, Tulsey town—Tulsa—struck oil. By 1910, the population had soared to 18,182; 14 years later Tulsa would be a prosperous city of 110,000 inhabitants. Not everybody got rich, of course. But the career of one man was a fair index to Tulsa's success. James J. McGraw arrived as a poor boy in the land rush of '93, and he rose with the town to become president of a bank, ensconced in offices in a 12-story skyscraper, doing an annual business of $40 million.

Even more spectacular was the growth of a planned city on the banks of the Calumet River in northern Indiana. In 1905, the site was 12.5 square miles of wasteland—rolling sand dunes covered with scrub oak. But late that year the city's namesake, Judge Elbert H. Gary, chairman of the board of United States Steel, poked a manicured finger at a map and told his directors, "This will be our metropolis. We'll build near the railroad junction of Chicago, where acres of land can be had almost for the asking, midway between the ore regions of the North and the coal regions of the South and East." The analysis was faultless and the city of Gary was christened before it was born.

The company's efforts soon proved once again that nothing could prevent American money and technology from working miracles. A bothersome river was moved a hundred yards. Great mechanical diggers chewed a mile-long harbor back from Lake Michigan; the major site was raised 15 feet with fill pumped in from the lake bottom. As railroad connections were forged, the jagged outlines of steel mills and foundries and tinplate plants rose against the sky. The final product was ready in July 1908. With proper ceremony, the first ore boat unloaded its cargo in Gary harbor and set the mills thundering. By 1910, Gary was an efficient corporative barony with a population of 16,802. That was Progress.

Or was it? A world of subtle difference separated true progress from mere change, and more and more Americans pondered the dimensions of that world as the decade wore on. Were urban phenomena like Gary and Tulsa and New York better places of habitation than the small town of Columbus, Indiana, or were they—as several grimly realistic novelists insisted—misbegotten work centers whose ugliness appalled the eye and whose labors crushed the human spirit with the mindless repetition of a single act on the production line? Did all their labor-saving, product-multiplying devices really improve the quality of American life? And was the work and wealth of modern industry divided equitably?

On this last count, the opponents of the status quo had a great deal to say. Muckraking journalists published angry exposés and backed their demands for reform with disturbing statistics. The average annual earnings of industrial workers in 1900 was a subsistence wage of less than $490; included in that figure were some 1.7 million children who labored for as little as 25 cents a day. One citizen out of eight lived in dire poverty in festering slums and perished of disease at about twice the rate of modest-income groups. In short, the reformers charged that labor was being exploited by an oligarchy of capitalists who lived in idle ostentation on annual incomes of many millions. The Very Rich said little in rebuttal, but one plutocrat did their cause no good by declaring arrogantly, "We own America; we got it, God knows how, but we intend to keep it."

Along these lines a battle was joined that would develop into a national crisis of social conscience. America's sense of justice and humanity, its treasured precept of equal opportunity for all, its jealously guarded tradition of free enterprise—all were called sharply into question. A free-swinging article in the Atlanta *Constitution* went so far as to say: "Government is no longer a vehicle for the enforcement of human rights but an agency for the furtherance of commercial interests."

Slowly, painfully, citizens faced up to the great civic work of 20th Century America: to make government more responsive to the needs and aspirations of the people; to reduce the discrepancies between lofty ideals and expedient practices, between good intentions and driving ambitions. That work had barely begun when the decade drew to a close. But it did begin. And *that* was Progress.

Yet if the sense of urgency was slow to grow, it was only natural to the time. For the great majority of people, the decade was a golden interlude, a long, comfortable moment before the good young days vanished completely and modern times arrived at full tide. Americans believed the judgments that confirmed their personal experience: That the human condition "is immensely improved and continually improving"; that "To stay in place in this country, you must keep moving"; that the average U.S. citizen possessed, and should enjoy, "the large cheerful average of health and success." It was generally true. Life for Americans from 1900 to 1910 was mellow and quite secure, full of vigor, savor and fascination. All they had to do was go out and live it.

A cartoonist's fantasy in 1901 included, among other items, 150-mile-per-hour trains and home ice-making machines—all by the end of the 20th Century.

A Man's World

The men of the Trident Boat Club of Manchester, New Hampshire, meet for an impromptu band concert.

The Master Sex

The relative positions to be assumed by man and woman in the working out of our civilization were assigned long ago by a higher intelligence than ours.

GROVER CLEVELAND

In any confrontation between the sexes, it was a foregone conclusion that men would come out ahead. For one thing, according to the 1900 census, men outnumbered women by more than a million and a half. But masculine supremacy went far beyond mere numbers. Like ex-President Grover Cleveland, every red-blooded American male was convinced that the sex he belonged to was innately superior.

The entire country, in fact, from the logging camps of Oregon to the U.S. Senate—with its convenient cuspidors—was seemingly arranged by men for their own satisfaction. Men ran the nation's business, cast its votes and produced most of its art and literature. They were, in theory at least, complete masters of their households, dispensing justice and wisdom to their families like Oriental potentates.

Along with their exalted status, men reserved special rights and privileges. Not only did they ban ladies from voting booths, they also kept them out of clubs, restaurants, saloons and tobacco shops. In some states an unescorted female might, by law, be refused a meal at a restaurant or a room at a hotel, and in 1904 one particularly audacious young lady was arrested and put in jail in New York City for smoking a cigarette in public.

While men called the tune, they also worked hard to pay the piper. Most men labored at least 10 hours a day, six days a week. An office worker was usually at his stool by eight o'clock, a factory hand at his bench by seven. Both would remain there until five-thirty or six, when they would trudge home to pipe, slippers and the affectionate ministrations of wife and children. All for an average weekly pay of less than $12.

In the confident mood of the first decade, however, most men were robustly certain that the opportunity to strike it rich lay just around the corner. With hard work and a bit of luck they might, like the Horatio Alger heroes, rise from clerk to president of the company. As good men, in an age of male superiority, they deserved no less.

But whether he was a bank teller or a board chairman, the American male usually managed to fit himself out in a style that was suitable to a member of the privileged sex. He acquired clothing and accessories—such as the fancy shirts, silk hats, matchboxes and other articles shown at right and on the following pages—that solidly proclaimed his membership in the world of men.

Sartorial artifacts of the men's world of 1900 included detachable collar and cuffs, pocket watches, a silk hat, eyeglasses in a silver case and a silver-headed cane.

DAMSCHINSKY'S
LIQUID
Hair Dye

NO LEAD!

GUARANTEED.

The Dandy's Gear

The average man used an impressive array of grooming devices (above), to keep his hair sleek, his face smooth and his moustache trim. The most essential item was a folding, straight-edged razor with a wood or ivory handle (foreground, on top of mirror), which he honed on a leather strop (left, hanging from oak shaving cabinet). Using a brush of soft badger hair (on cup, foreground), he worked up a lather in a china shaving mug, which was often ornamented with a personal insignia. The mugs in the cabinet include one bearing the owner's initials, another (middle of the center shelf) decorated with the emblem of the owner's fraternal organization, the Elks. After-shave lotion was kept in colorful glass bottles; cologne bottles were occasionally protected in boxwood cases (near blue after-shave bottles). For the hair and moustache, there was pomade (top shelf, at left)—and sometimes hair dye to preserve the youthful look that all men desired.

The Master's Toys

Most men's pleasures were fairly simple—a good cigar, a tot of whiskey, a poker game with friends—but the paraphernalia that went with them (right) was often elaborate. Cigar cutters took the shape of guillotines (rear center). There were oil lamps that both clipped and lighted a fragrant Havana (center, inscribed with an ad for Blaine Cigars). The majority of men chewed plug tobacco, and prided themselves on their talent for scoring a bull's-eye in a shiny brass spittoon (right, holding cards). But cigars and pipes, from simple briars to elegantly carved meerschaums (foreground), were almost as popular. Whiskey was often kept in fancy crystal decanters that could be locked into a portable case (right, rear), or in handy breast-pocket flasks shaped like cigars (center foreground). Poker chips and counters for various other card and dice games ranged from conventional disks to rectangular counters and ivory fish (right foreground).

Rudy Sohn's Barber Shop in Junction City, Kansas, with its reclining chairs and rows of shaving mugs on the wall, exuded an air of solid, masculine comfort.

Manly Retreats

"There is something mentally enervating in feminine companionship," advised *The Cosmopolitan* in 1905, and so "the genuine man feels that he must go off alone or with other men, out in the open air, as it were, roughing it among the rough, as a mental tonic." The spirit, if not the letter, of that statement was dogma at the time. Most men sought the society of other males in less rugged circumstances, in the comfortable, for-men-only atmosphere of barbershops, clubs and saloons. A turn-of-the-century barbershop was much more than a place to get a haircut. It was a retreat where, amid the reek of cigar fumes and bay rum, men would congregate to browse through the spicy pages of the *Police Gazette*, ogle the ladies who hurried past the door, and wait for a 15-cent shave.

Even more impregnable to women were the men's clubs. For the rich and wellborn, there were such exclusive establishments as New York City's august Union League Club, whose major asset, according to one member, was the fact that "no women, no dogs, no Democrats, no reporters" could be found there. But most clubs were a good deal more proletarian. The average man could join sporting societies, volunteer fire companies, municipal bands and marching societies, and gourmandizing fraternities with such fancy names as the Honorable John McSorley Pickle, Beefsteak, Baseball Nine and Chowder Club, which held raucous clambakes on an island in the East River in New York.

The most democratic gathering places of all were the saloons. There were at least 100,000 of these in the country, supplied by 3,000 breweries and distilleries. It is a fact of record that in Boston and Chicago, half the male population paid a daily visit to favored neighborhood bars. Part of the saloon's appeal was camaraderie, but the main attraction was the whiskey. So important was this commodity that on one occasion, when a supplier drew up to the door of a saloon with 20 large kegs of whiskey and a few small sacks of flour, one customer dryly commented, "Now what in hell does he think we're going to do with all that flour."

The Cosmopolitan Saloon in Telluride, Colorado, featured roulette and a mahogany bar, which served whiskey as raw and rugged as the men who drank it.

With an appropriate set of props—shotguns, rifles, bottles, hounds and a papier-mâché rabbit—the Skeet Club of Fall Creek, Wisconsin, sits for an official portrait.

Number One fire-eaters, members of the fire department of Woodbine, New Jersey, assemble around patriarchal chief.

Lodge brothers of the Independent Order of Odd Fellows at Kerkhoven, Minnesota, display their ceremonial regalia.

Volunteer fire companies, like this one from Longmont, Colorado, often spent as much time training for races (above) with other towns as drilling for fires.

Crowned in laurel wreaths, an Olympian assemblage honors the theatrical promoter Harrison Grey Fiske (front row, third from left) at a lush dinner about 1901.

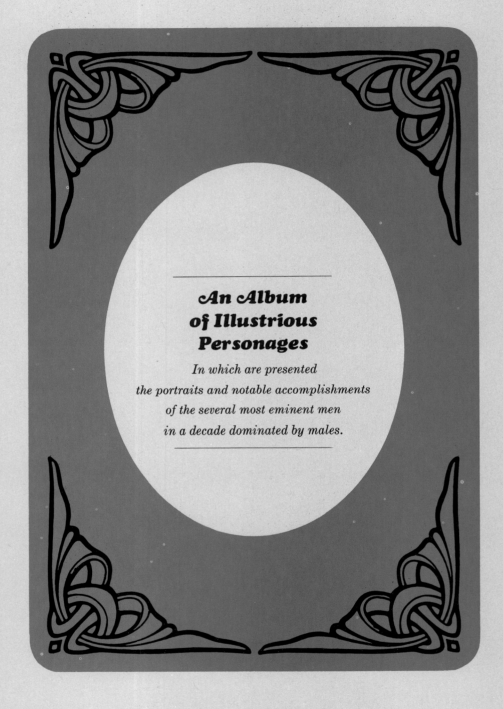

An Album
of Illustrious
Personages

*In which are presented
the portraits and notable accomplishments
of the several most eminent men
in a decade dominated by males.*

Arctic explorer *Robert E. Peary drove a dogsled 400 miles from his ship to become the first man to stand at the North Pole. He reached it on April 6, 1909, in cold so intense that a flask of brandy carried under his parka froze solid. He marked the spot with the Stars and Stripes and the colors of the Red Cross, of the Navy League, of the Daughters of the American Revolution and of Delta Kappa Epsilon (his college fraternity). Returning to civilization, Peary cabled his wife: "Have made good at last. I have the old Pole."*

Military man *General Leonard Wood was the stern symbol of a strong Amer-ica during the country's colonial expansion. First a practicing physician, then winner of a Congressional Medal of Honor in action against the Apach-es in 1886, he later commanded U.S. troops during the Spanish-American War. Subsequently, as military governor of Cuba, he directed the fight against yellow fever and provided for the uplift of the lives, education and government of the native population with a healthy serving of Anglo-Saxon civilization.*

Press czar *William Randolph Hearst ushered in mass-circulation newspapers with sensationalism. After initial success with the San Francisco "Examiner," he bought the failing New York "Morning Journal" in 1895 and made it the model of yellow journalism. Through the lavish use of photographs, splashy headlines, colored comics, a saber-rattling editorial policy and some juicy scandals, he soon upped its circulation to an unprecedented 1.5 million copies— thus bringing more news to more Americans than any publisher before him.*

Minority champion *William Jennings Bryan led the underdog Democratic Party for almost two decades with a combination of shrewd cloakroom deals and compelling oratory. He ran three times for President but was beaten by Republicans McKinley and Taft. Even in defeat he was a formidable fighter for such lost causes as silver-based currency, attacking the gold standard with broadsides of Biblical locution: "You shall not press down upon the brow of labor this crown of thorns; you shall not crucify mankind upon a cross of gold."*

Beau ideal *Richard Harding Davis personified masculinity and derring-do. Novelist, journalist, man-about-town, he was known as the top war correspondent of his era. However, his flair for dramatic reporting was more than matched by his dashing appearance—square-jawed, clean shaven, stylish even on the battlefield. His personality was a strange mixture of vanity and self-mockery. "What I like most in men," he said, is the ability "to sit opposite a mirror at dinner and not look in it"—an ability he himself did not possess.*

Kingpin banker *J. Pierpont Morgan was the most powerful financier in American history. The very "embodiment of power and purpose," according to a fellow businessman, he used his uncanny business sense and awesome presence to create the world's largest corporation, U.S. Steel. Later, he singlehandedly saved the country from financial collapse in the panic of 1907—by holding 125 leading New York financiers under lock and key in his palatial library near Madison Avenue until they produced the capital to stave off disaster.*

Leading educator *Booker T. Washington rose from slavery to found America's first college for Negro teachers, Tuskegee Institute in Alabama. Though resentment against Negro advancement ran high, President Theodore Roosevelt openly described the Negro leader as the South's most distinguished citizen. When the President asked him to dinner at the White House, most Southerners were scandalized. In the face of such bigotry, Washington felt no bitterness. "I shall never permit myself to stoop so low as to hate any man," he said.*

The man of the decade, *President Theodore Roosevelt was the living embodiment of the optimism and energy of the country's mood. During his seven and a half years of vigorous, personal leadership, from 1901 to 1909, he wielded the powers of the Presidency as no man had done before. Roosevelt called his crusade the Square Deal, and the people loved it. They loved him for himself, too. "I have never known another person so vital," wrote author and editor William Allen White, speaking for the nation, "nor another man so dear."*

The American Colossus

Among the many notable men of his time, Theodore Roosevelt—soldier, statesman, author, adventurer and advocate of the strenuous life—stood out above all others and left an unmistakable stamp on America. It was not physical stature, certainly, that made Roosevelt appear such a dominant figure. Dumpy-looking, his eyes heavily spectacled, a toothy smile protruding from under a walrus moustache, he cut an almost comical figure, somewhat like a cartoonist's rendition of an early Colonel Blimp. Neither was he a giant merely because of his birth—he was the son of a patrician Dutch family from New York City; nor because of his political office, the Presidency. It was rather the dynamic force of his presence, together with his awesome energy, that made the ebullient Teddy stand larger in people's minds than any other man of his time. "His personality so crowds the room," said a friend, "that the walls are worn thin and threaten to burst outward."

Everything about T.R. seemed bigger than life. He drank his coffee, with seven lumps of sugar, from a cup that, according to his eldest son, Teddy Jr., was "more in the nature of a bathtub." When he spoke, with a high-pitched, staccato bark, he became a "human volcano, roaring as only a human volcano can roar!—leading the laughter and singing and shouting, like a boy out of school, pounding the table with both noisy fists." He walked with such a fierce, determined stride that most people had to break into a dogtrot to keep up with him. "I always believe in going hard at everything," he wrote his son Kermit. Nothing dampened his enthusiasm for rough-and-tumble. During a fox hunt in 1885, he fell off his horse and broke his arm. He remounted, finished the hunt, went out to dinner in the evening and the next day tramped through the woods for three hours. "I like to drink the wine of life with brandy in it," he said.

This same unflagging vitality drove Roosevelt to the front line of public life. At age 24, he leaped into politics as a crusading Republican state assemblyman from New York City, determined to clean up political abuses in both parties. As New York City's police commissioner, he packed a pistol and patrolled the city streets to make sure his policemen kept busy catching criminals. With the outbreak of the Spanish-American War in 1898, he traded in his job as Assistant Secretary of the Navy to lead a volunteer cavalry regiment, the Rough Riders, in a daredevil charge up San Juan Hill in Cuba. "I don't want to be in office during war," he said; "I want to be at the front."

Teddy's swashbuckling approach to public life often infuriated old-line politicians. The Republican national chairman, Mark Hanna, called him "that damned cowboy," and on the eve of T.R.'s election as Vice President under William McKinley in 1900, Hanna exclaimed in dismay, "Don't any of you realize there's only one life between that madman and the Presidency?"

Only six months after McKinley's inauguration, Hanna's fears were realized. In September 1901, an assassin's bullet took McKinley's life, and Teddy rattled by wagon down the trail from a mountain lodge in the Adirondacks to become, at age 42, the youngest President in American history.

Roosevelt plunged into the adventure of being President with the enthusiasm of a small boy embarking on a hayride. "You must always remember," said a British diplomat, "that the President is about six." But Teddy's accomplishments were man-sized. He acted to curb the power of the nation's huge trade monopolies and financial trusts—"malefactors of great wealth," as he called them. He arbitrated labor disputes, reformed railroad rates, pushed through a pure food and drug law and plucked 148 million acres of forest land from under the noses of lumbermen to create national parks. Wielding his famous "big stick" in foreign affairs, he battered down stubborn diplomatic obstacles to build the Panama Canal.

Inevitably, Roosevelt's energetic policies made him enemies. But though T.R. claimed he did not "care a rap for 'popularity' as such," the American people refused to believe him. His public appearances drew enthusiastic crowds. "Whenever he is in the neighborhood," wrote a commentator, "the public can no more look the other way than a small boy can turn his head from a circus parade followed by a steam calliope." Campaigning in 1904 on his platform of a Square Deal for every American, Teddy was re-elected for a second term by the largest plurality amassed until then by a Presidential candidate.

Roosevelt was more than an energetic but shallow demagogue in a cowboy hat. His intellectual interests seemed to touch the whole spectrum of human knowledge. "Whether the subject of the moment was political economy, the Greek drama, tropical fauna or flora, the Irish sagas, protective coloration in nature, metaphysics, the technique of football, or postfuturist painting," wrote the English statesman Viscount Lee, "he was equally at home with the experts." T.R. was himself such an au-

thority on North American animal life that the professional zoologists at the Smithsonian Institution once called on him to identify a mystifying specimen of mammal in their collection.

Roosevelt's passion for reading was virtually insatiable. He consumed books at the rate of two or three a day, and he himself wrote 24 of them—histories, biographies, descriptions of cattle ranching and big game hunting, scholarly studies on natural history, speeches, magazine articles and newspaper editorials. Sometimes his writing took on a rather moralistic tone; a friend once said, "If there is one thing more than any other for which I admire you, Theodore, it is your original discovery of the Ten Commandments." But the following excerpts, despite a certain pompous sense of right, reveal the determination, the vigor and the intelligence that made up the spirit of the decade's biggest man.

Having been a sickly boy, with no natural bodily prowess, and having lived much at home, I was at first quite unable to hold my own when thrown into contact with other boys of rougher antecedents. I was nervous and timid. Yet from reading of the people I admired I felt a great admiration for men who were fearless and who could hold their own in the world, and I had a great desire to be like them.

I am only an average man but, by George, I work harder at it than the average man.

It was still the Wild West in those days, the far West. We knew toil and hardship and hunger and thirst; and we saw men die violent deaths as they worked among the horses and cattle, or fought evil feuds with one another; but we felt the beat of hardy life in our veins, and ours was the glory of work and the joy of living.

I have scant use for the type of sportsmanship which consists merely in looking on at the feats of someone else.

There are no words that can tell the hidden spirit of the wilderness, that can reveal its mystery, its melancholy, and its charm. There is delight in the hardy life of the open, in long rides rifle in hand, in the thrill of the fight with dangerous game. Apart from this, yet mingled with it, is the strong attraction of the silent places, of the large tropic moons, and

the splendor of the new stars; where the wanderer sees the awful glory of sunrise and sunset in the wide waste spaces of the earth, unworn of man, and changed only by the slow change of the ages through time everlasting.

We demand that big business give the people a square deal; in return we must insist that when any one engaged in big business honestly endeavors to do right he shall himself be given a square deal.

There is a homely adage which runs, "Speak softly and carry a big stick; you will go far."

Do not hit at all if it can be avoided, but never hit softly.

I wish to preach, not the doctrine of ignoble ease, but the doctrine of the strenuous life, the life of toil and effort, of labor and strife; to preach that highest form of success which comes, not to the man who desires mere easy peace, but to the man who does not shrink from danger, or from bitter toil, and who out of these wins the splendid ultimate triumph.

The White House is a bully pulpit.

For unflagging interest and enjoyment, a household of children, if things go reasonably well, certainly makes all other forms of success and achievement lose their importance by comparison.

Roosevelt sits for a 1903 family portrait with his wife, Edith, and children (from left): Quentin, 5; Ted, 15; Archie, 9; Alice, 19; Kermit, 13; and Ethel, 11.

Father of the First Family

Despite his eagerness for action and adventure, Teddy Roosevelt, like most other males of the decade, was very much a family man. He had six children, whom he managed to line up for the solemn portrait above. But the normal mood of the first family was about as sedate as a public school recess. There were baseball games on the White House lawn, tag in the hallways and a menagerie of assorted pets that included dogs, rabbits, flying squirrels, a badger and a small black bear. According to one seasoned retainer, it was "the wildest scramble in the history of the White House."

Roosevelt, far from restraining the activities of his children, often took part himself. He engaged them in wrestling bouts, pillow fights and football games. While at Sagamore Hill, the Roosevelt summer home near New York City, he took them on tramps through the woods and joined them in "romps" in the hayloft, although he admitted that it seemed "rather odd for a stout, elderly President to be bouncing over hay-ricks."

Roosevelt's constant delight in the doings of his offspring is reflected in his letters and other writings. The excerpts that accompany the photographs on the following pages reveal a fatherly pride that sometimes eclipsed even his pride in his wide-ranging public achievements.

"I don't think that any family has ever enjoyed the White House more than we have," Roosevelt wrote. Above, the two youngest children, Archie and Quentin, indulge in a favorite pastime—standing reveille with the White House guards.

Quentin, the baby, shows his pony to a White House officer. "He had one tumble," wrote T.R., "which, he remarked philosophically, did not hurt him any more than when I whacked him with a sofa cushion in one of our pillow fights."

Archie, "a most warm-hearted, loving, cunning little goose," was considered to be the best-natured and most outgoing of the rambunctious Roosevelt brood. He had hundreds of friends of all ages, including this solemn White House sentry.

"Archie and Quentin are great playmates," their father wrote of the two youngsters, who here try photography. "Quenty-quee has cast off the trammels of the nursery and become a most fearless though very good-tempered little boy."

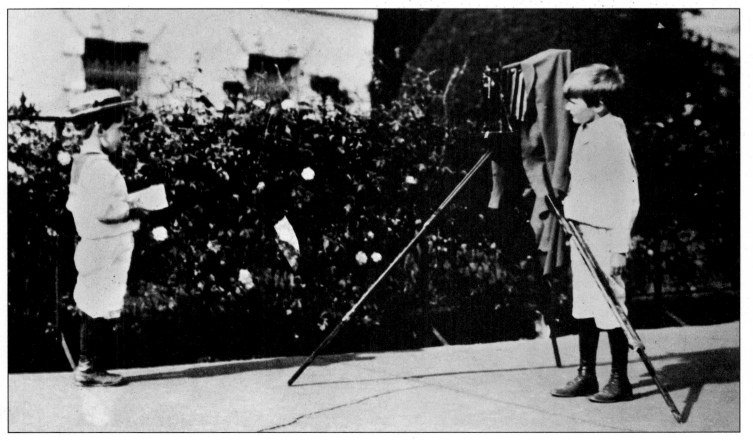

Of the six children, the most willful were the girls. Before one stint of baby-sitting with his younger daughter, Ethel, Roosevelt wrote in mock despair, "I have gloomy forebodings that after a brief struggle Ethel will take care of me."

Kermit, here holding his terrier, Allan, was a dreamy-eyed, introspective boy. When still very young, he was entranced by the evening sky and kept asking T.R., who he thought could do anything, to "get the moon, Father," and bring it to him.

Alice, the elder daughter, led such an active social life that T.R. complained she "only makes her appearance well after noon having been up until all hours dancing the night before."

*Like the others, Ted, the eldest boy, loved pets. One of his favorites
was a large bird named Eli, "the most gorgeous macaw," which his father
claimed had "a bill that I think could bite through boiler plate."*

Archie's favorite mascot was a badger named Josiah. When not holding Josiah on his lap, Archie would wear out his stockings crawling after the pet, "whose temper," wrote the President, "was short but whose nature was fundamentally friendly."

The antics of Quentin and Archie, below, blowing soap bubbles on the lawn at Sagamore Hill, never ceased to delight the President. "Archie and Quentin are just as cunning as they can be," he commented in a glow of fatherly affection.

Quentin, like his older brothers, was constantly acquiring pets, including a hutchful of rabbits, which, his father noted, "he brought in while we were at lunch yesterday, explaining that they were 'the valuablest kind, with pink eyes.' "

"There could be no healthier and pleasanter place in which to bring up children than that nook of old-time America around Sagamore Hill," wrote T. R., who joins in a football game at the country place that served as the summer White House.

Immigrants with baggage and identification tags land on Ellis Island, New York.

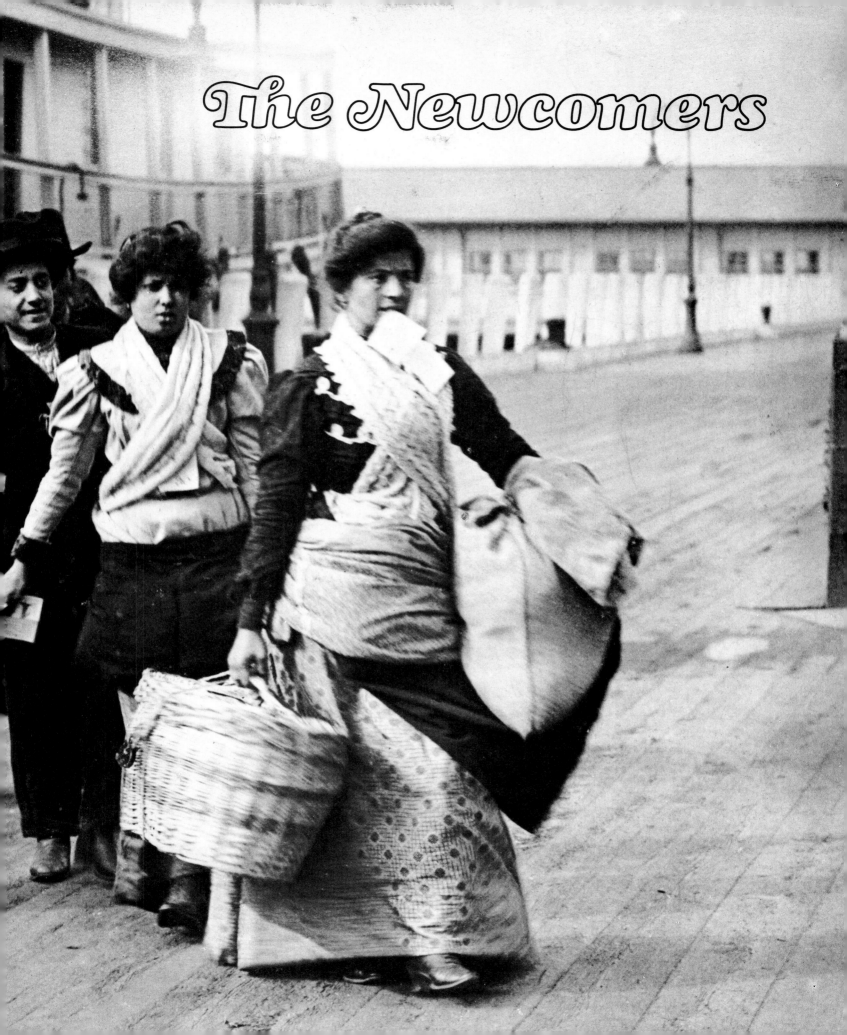

The Newcomers

The Immigrants' Ordeal

Give me your tired, your poor, your huddled masses yearning to breathe free. Send
... the homeless, tempest-tossed, to me, I lift my lamp beside the golden door!
INSCRIPTION ON THE STATUE OF LIBERTY

The scum of creation has been dumped on us. The most dangerous and corrupting
hordes of the Old World have invaded us. The vice and crime which they have planted
in our midst are sickening and terrifying.
NATIVE-BORN POLITICIAN THOMAS WATSON

"Becoming an American," wrote a grateful but case-hardened immigrant, "is a spiritual adventure of the most volcanic variety." Heedless of such cautionings, some nine million immigrants came knocking at America's "golden door" between 1900 and 1910. Many were so poor that they could barely scrape together their fare in steerage—sums as small as $12 for the voyage from Italy. But all were irresistibly drawn by the conviction that in America they would find what the old country had denied them.

What they found in America severely tested the immigrants' faith—and their courage and stamina as well. For most of the newcomers, the ordeal of Americanization began on a bleak scrap of real estate in New York harbor, Ellis Island. In 1907, more than a million immigrants poured through the island's overtaxed processing facilities. Once admitted to the "Land of Opportunity," most newcomers were doomed to years of toil (12-hour days and six- or seven-day weeks), at subsistence pay (an average of less than $12.50 a week), in the garment-making sweatshops of New York, in the coal mines of Wilkes-Barre, in the spinning mills of Fall River and the grimy factories and slaughterhouses of Pittsburgh, Chicago and other Midwestern cities.

Though the immigrants were welcomed by Americans of good will, they also met with plain and fancy prejudice. Xenophobic natives ridiculed their alien ways, and regarded them as subhuman animals. Men as influential as Senator Henry Cabot Lodge lent prestige to bigotry by insisting that the latter-day immigrants were inferior peoples whose prolific issue threatened the very foundations of Anglo-American civilization. No less a savant than Francis A. Walker, president of the Massachusetts Institute of Technology, was so seized by prejudice that he pronounced the newcomers "beaten men from beaten races; representing the worst failures in the struggle for existence. They have none of the ideas and aptitudes which belong to those who are descended from the tribes that met under the oak trees of old Germany to make laws and choose chieftains."

Disillusioned by bigotry and poverty, many immigrants gave up and returned home; 395,000 departed in 1908 alone. But the vast majority persevered. "Their hearts," said sociologist Charles B. Spahr, "cannot be alienated. The ideals, the opportunities of our democracy change the immigrants into a new order of men."

Mother and child, awaiting admission on Ellis Island, New York, are marked as immigrants by peasant garb—and the expression of hope, fear and stoic patience.

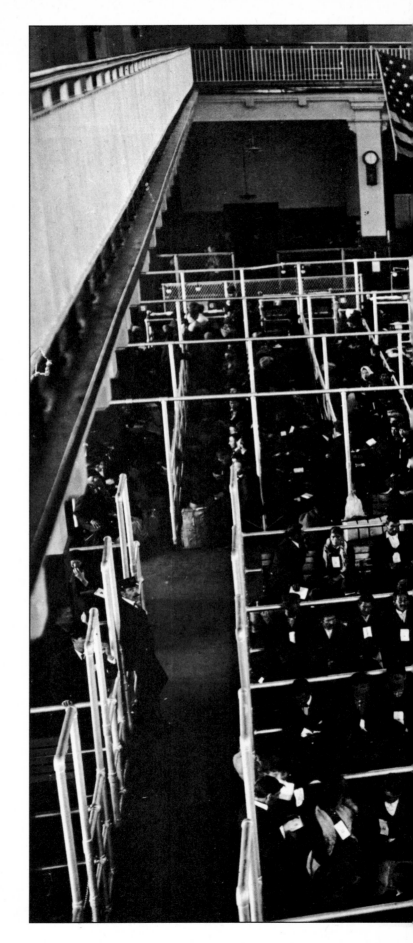

Among the hordes to arrive in America in that climactic year of immigration, 1907, was a small boy of 10 from Italy, Edward Corsi, who later became U.S. Commissioner of Immigration and Naturalization for New York. Corsi's tour of duty as an official on Ellis Island kept fresh the memory of his own childhood arrival there; years later he recalled *(below)* the October day that brought him and his family from shipboard in the haze-hung harbor to their new home in an East Side tenement.

---

*M*ountains!" *I cried to my brother. "Look at them!" "They're strange," he said. "Why don't they have snow on them?" He was craning his neck and standing on tiptoe to stare through the haze at the New York skyline.*

A small boat, the "General Putnam" of the Immigration Service, carried us from the pier to Ellis Island. We took our places in the long line and went submissively through the routine of answering interpreters' questions and receiving medical examinations. We were in line early so we avoided the necessity of staying overnight, an ordeal which my mother had long been dreading. Soon we were permitted to pass through America's gateway.

Crossing the harbor on the ferry, I was first struck by the fact that American men did not wear beards. In contrast with my own countrymen I thought they looked almost like women. I felt we were superior to them. I saw my first negro.

Carrying our baggage, we walked across lower Manhattan and then climbed the steps leading to one of these marvellous trains. On this train I saw a Chinaman, queue and all! It had been a day of breath-taking surprises. I decided that anything might be true in this strange country.

Penned up in national groups, immigrants wait on Ellis Island. On an average day, 4,000 newcomers were processed, but 2,000 of them had to stay overnight.

Old World Beauties Greeted by American Bachelors

Under banner headlines like the one above, newspapers from coast to coast spread the joyful word that on September 27, 1907, a steamship had docked in New York with a spectacular cargo from Europe—1,002 unmarried girls. The Old World beauties came ashore to a hectic welcome. As photographers recorded their smiles *(right)*, the ladies were besieged by a crowd of bachelors and regaled by a band playing "Cupid's Garden" and "I Want You, Honey, Yes I Do." Here, in excerpts from the New York *World*, are details of the happy landing.

No marriage mart of the Orient where brides were merchandise ever presented so bewitching a picture as the decks of the "Baltic" yesterday when 1002 beauties, colleens from Ireland, lasses from Scotland, maidens from Wales, girls from England and blondes from Scandinavia, rosy, dimpled and roguish eyed, marriageable every one, stood there, fascinated by their first glimpse of the New World.

"I like tall men and blondes," said Susan Thompson frankly, and then her companions all screamed and Susan laughed until she could hardly speak. "I have read much about Americans making good husbands."

Miss Agnes McGirr's home is in Edinburgh. "I want a man with dark hair," she chirped. "A city man? No, a farmer. A man who is making $1000 a year will do. That isn't too much to ask in this country is it? How old? Thirty. He has some sense, then."

"They tell me," remarked Nellie O'Brien from Loch Crae, *Tipperary, "that there are no men in Pittsburgh but millionaires. I'm going there, and it's soon I'll be riding in my own carriage, I suppose."*

As for the accomplishments of these girls, no list would be long enough to enumerate them, and no rash man so ungallant as to abridge them. They can cook, sing and play the piano, scrub, take care of a house and mind children, milk cows, raise chickens, weed garden beds, go to market, sew, patch and knit, make cheese and butter, pickle cucumbers and drive cattle.

No wonder when he heard they were coming a farmer out in Kansas wrote: "John Lee, Vice-President of the Merchantile Marine Steamship Company: Dear Sir: I am a widower with a couple of married daughters, but I want a new wife, who is to come out here to Kansas the minute the 'Baltic' gets in. There is only one other house near mine. She can tell my house by the green shutters. Tell her not to make a mistake."

Doing "home work" in the dreary confines of their New York tenement, an Italian immigrant family earns a precarious living by making artificial flowers.

Hard Lessons for Greenhorns

Bewildered at first by their strange new country, most immigrants huddled together in urban enclaves of their own. But once they had entered the Germantowns and Jewtowns and Little Italys, their fine new freedoms were whittled away by the sharp edge of poverty.

Each ethnic slum was a tiny world that clutched at its denizens, holding them to a few filthy streets, markets and sweatshops. Seldom did the overworked laborer or his child-burdened wife have the will to venture a couple of miles to the wonderland of theaters and department stores. Elderly residents on the upper floors of tenements hesitated to attempt the ramshackle stairs; some did not leave their dingy flats for years.

The degradation of the slumdwellers triggered angry volleys from reform-minded muckrakers. Journalist Jacob Riis, himself an immigrant from Denmark, presented grim photographs and stories of festering tenements and their disease-ridden inmates; he warned his readers that "In the battle of the slum we win or we perish. There is no middle ground." Novelist Frank Norris, reporting on the Pennsylvania coal fields, quoted a miner's opinion of the lot of local immigrants: "They don't live no better than dogs." Norris disagreed. Their existence, he said, was much worse: "They live in houses built of sheet-iron, and boards, about fifteen feet square and sunk about three feet in the ground. Of course there is but one room, and in this room the family—anywhere from six to ten humans—cooks, eats and sleeps."

Despite the long-range benefits of such exposés, the immigrants received little practical help and almost no immediate improvement in their condition. Happily, there were exceptional cases, and a few city governments took steps to make life easier for the poor. Tom L. Johnson (*overleaf*), the benevolent mayor of Cleveland, Ohio, introduced cheap public transportation and built parks, playgrounds and public baths to help brighten the dreariness of slum life. But in most other places, immigrants were forced to rely upon themselves. Banding together to seek strength in numbers, they joined religious brotherhoods, community welfare

Drab houses crowd a byway in Chicago's grimmest ghetto, the Maxwell Street area. This section was occupied successively by groups of Irish, Jews and Negroes.

associations, labor unions and local political clubs.

Politically, most of the newcomers were inexperienced and naive; they spent years learning how to use the American party system to make government responsive to their needs. In the interim, many became the clients —and the victims—of machine politicians, who, although they did offer some leadership and protection, nevertheless set records for venality and greed. Perhaps the greediest of all was tough William Flinn, a Pittsburgh boss who made several fortunes in high-level graft; when Flinn died in 1924, he left an estate of more than $11 million. But even lesser ward bosses amassed millions in small "donations" from shopkeepers, criminals and companies angling for business with the city.

Thus any crafty boss had plenty of money to spend, and he spent it liberally down in the wards whence came his power. In New York City, with its immigrant-crowded slums, the casting of bread upon the waters brought manifold returns to the Tammany organization of boss Charles F. Murphy. One of Murphy's lieutenants, George W. Plunkitt, was an expert on philanthropy. "If a family is burned out," explained this rich and genial grafter, "I don't ask whether they are Republicans or Democrats. I just get quarters for them, buy clothes for them if their clothes were burned up, and fix them up till they get things runnin' again. Who can tell how many votes these fires bring me?"

Because Flinn and many other bosses were immigrants with big immigrant followings, bigoted natives held the newcomers responsible for political corruption. But the muckraking champions of the hapless immigrant put bossism and corruption in proper perspective. "The boss," said Riis, "is like measles, a distemper of a self-governing people's infancy." Lincoln Steffens, investigating municipal corruption for a series in *McClure's* magazine, discovered that New York and Chicago were well governed despite their immigrants, while Philadelphia, "the purest American community of all," was "the most hopeless." Steffens concluded: "The 'foreign element' excuse is one of the hypocritical lies that save us from the clear sight of ourselves."

The prejudice and scorn of natives drove many immigrants in upon themselves and hardened them. However, most of the younger immigrants, and almost all

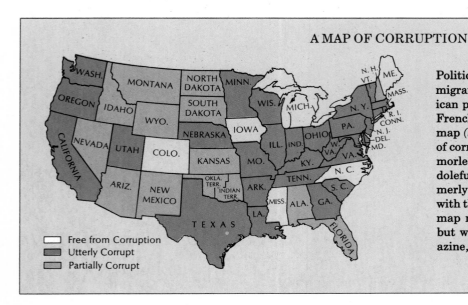

A MAP OF CORRUPTION

Free from Corruption
Utterly Corrupt
Partially Corrupt

Political corruption, sometimes blamed on the immigrants, touched off loud explosions in the American press—and a curious echo far off in France. A French editor used wild imagination to produce a map (*left*) purporting to show accurately the degree of corruption throughout the United States. This humorless work of cartography was accompanied by a doleful prognosis for the U.S.: "The organism, formerly healthy, has become incontestably infected with the germs of contagious decay." The lugubrious map may have aroused serious concern in France, but when it was reproduced in an American magazine, readers were amused in spite of themselves.

The poor man's champion, Mayor Tom L. Johnson of Cleveland, glows among his constituents. His municipal reforms gave Cleveland a nationwide reputation.

of the second generation, sought to win acceptance by Americanization. They were pathetically eager to abandon Old World ways and dress, to speak English without an accent, to acquire American friends and manners. A Polish immigrant, gainfully employed in a Polish section but frustrated by the "foreign" environment, wrote a touching appeal to the Massachusetts Commission on Immigration: "I want live with american people, but where? Not in the country, because I want go in the city, free evening schools and lern. I'm looking for help. If somebody could give me another job between american people, help me live with them and lern english—and could tell me the best way how I can lern—it would be very, very good for me."

Ironically, the ideal of assimilation was responsible for the immigrant's ultimate tragedy. Some parents encouraged their children's efforts to Americanize. Others resisted with the full strength of their Old World authority. But in either case, the results were usually the same. Even before the children grew up and left home, they drifted away from the family, and the gap between the generations steadily widened.

Complete Americanization was the goal of Mary Antin, a gifted girl from Russia whose family settled in a Boston slum. With the father's encouragement, the children went their own way; Mary devoted herself to study and writing. She scored a grade-school triumph when her poem in praise of George Washington was published in the Boston *Herald*, and her father proudly distributed among friends all the papers he could buy. In the arrogance of her youthful fame, and with a faith in America that defied yet demanded explication, Mary wrote passionately, "It would have been amazing if I had stuck in the mire of the slum. By every law of my nature, I was bound to soar above it, to attain the fairer places that wait for every emancipated immigrant."

Mary Antin and countless fellow immigrants did escape from the slums into the American mainstream. But they left behind many others—people once as optimistic as they—to hopeless poverty and frustration.

Staring blankly, a young slum woman pauses in her crude kitchen amid evidence of defeat and despair: a broken faucet, an abandoned boot, a littered floor.

Orville Wright makes the first airplane flight, while brother Wilbur trots alongside.

A Decade of Ups and Downs

Aerial flight is one of that class of problems with which man can never cope.
SIMON NEWCOMB, 1903

Success assured. Keep quiet.
ORVILLE WRIGHT, 1903

In the year 1903, almost nobody believed that men would ever fly. Most people simply agreed with the noted astronomer, Simon Newcomb, when he said that it was just common sense to keep both feet firmly planted on the ground.

At least two men knew better. In December 1903, on a sandspit at Kitty Hawk, North Carolina, Orville and Wilbur Wright were putting the last touches on a "whopper flying machine" they had built at their bicycle shop in Dayton, Ohio, and shipped to Kitty Hawk for tests. Confident of success, Orville sent the telegram above to his father in Dayton urging secrecy. Then quite suddenly on December 17 it was done. The two brothers piloted their flimsy, jerry-built machine on a series of wobbly flights, the longest one lasting 59 seconds and covering 852 feet.

The next day, only two newspapers across the entire United States saw fit to carry the story. Other papers were still grousing over an earlier flight attempt that seemed to confirm the national suspicion that the sky was a place only for birds, angels and fools. Just nine days before Kitty Hawk, the secretary of the Smithsonian Institution, Samuel Langley, had tried to launch a winged contraption from the roof of a houseboat on the Potomac River in Washington, D.C. Langley, backed by a $50,000 grant from the War Department, had spent five years perfecting his machine. But while boatloads of reporters and government officials watched expectantly, the craft had left its catapult and plunged nose first (*opposite*) into the Potomac.

With the soggy demise of Langley's pioneering effort most people's interest in aviation took a nose dive. Not until 1908, after Wilbur and Orville demonstrated an improved version of their airplane to U.S. government officials, did the public awaken to the fact that men were truly flying. Then it seemed that everyone wanted to get into the air.

Across the country, inspired backyard aeronauts started building their own weird-looking contraptions, all designed to go the Wrights one better. Sportsmen and military daredevils mingled at fashionable air meets. As this whirl of airborne activity got under way, Wilbur Wright observed soberly that "the age of flight had come at last." Indeed it had, but there was still no agreement whatever (*following pages*) on the best way for man to stay aloft, now that he had finally gotten there.

A $50,000 disaster, Samuel Langley's airplane caught a wing tip on its catapult and broke apart in mid-air before plummeting into the Potomac River.

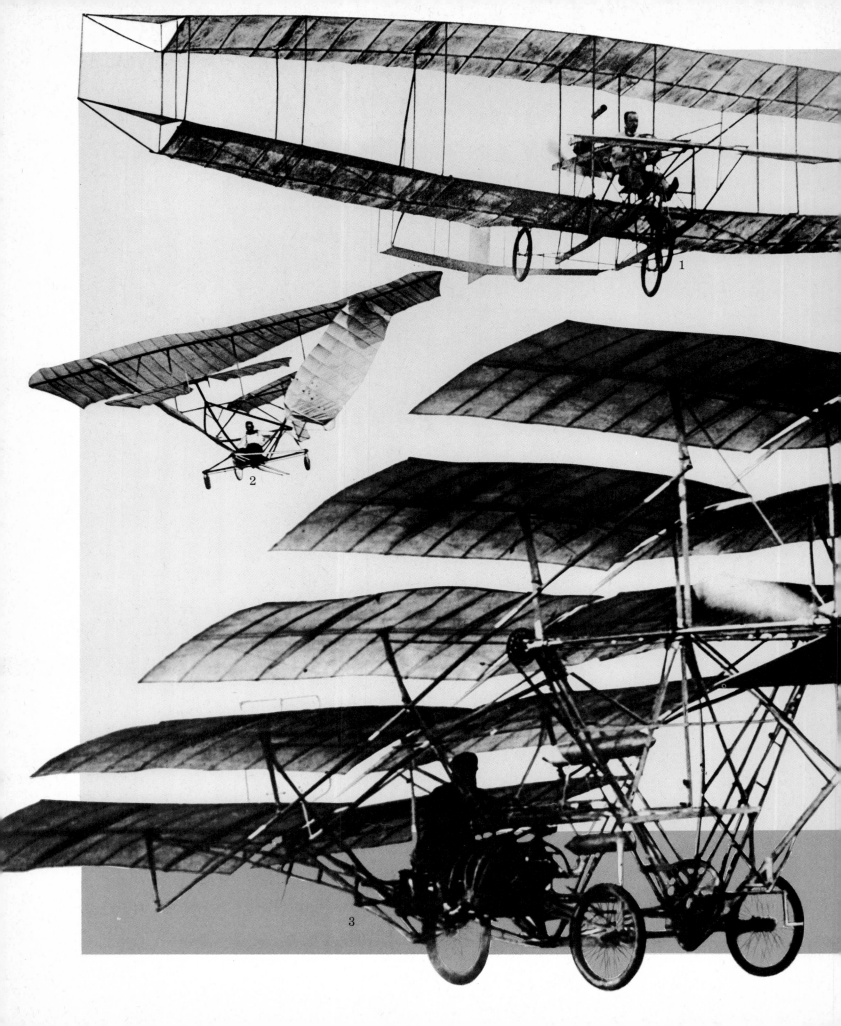

1

2

3

1. *Glenn Curtiss piloting his first plane, "June Bug," in 1908.*
2. *W. H. Martin takes off in his "Martinette" glider, 1909.*
3. *J. S. Zerbe's 1910 quintaplane failed to get off the ground.*
4. *Wilbur Wright piloting "Flyer" in a 1909 exhibition.*
5. *Clifton O. Hadley flies his homemade triplane, about 1910.*
6. *John A. D. McCurdy, 1908, taking off in his "Silver Dart."*

Despite its two imposing overhead rotors, this prototype helicopter hammered together by the blacksmith of Jetmore, Kansas, never made it off the town's main street.

The living image of a Halloween fantasy, Mrs. Cromwell Dixon guides a gasoline-powered dirigible pasted and screwed together by her 14-year-old son.

CROMWELL DIXON

MRS. DIXON

A Grand Old Gasbag

While newborn planes were staggering aloft, an even more unlikely type of aircraft began to drift across the American skies. It was called the dirigible, and it was a gas-filled, sausage-shaped balloon propelled by an engine. The most precocious of the various dirigible-builders of the decade was 14-year-old Cromwell Dixon of Columbus, Ohio. With the aid of a determined mother, Dixon designed and actually flew several airships, including one model that could be driven through the sky like a bicycle, by pedaling. In the following letter to *St. Nicholas* magazine, Dixon's proud mother describes the setbacks and successes of the youthful aeronaut.

Dear St. Nicholas   Columbus, Ohio
        As I attend to my son Cromwell's business, I will write you a few lines pertaining to his work, and also send you some very good photographs of Cromwell himself and his sky-bicycle and of his air-ship. Most people prefer the sky-bicycle, as it was the little fellow's own invention and he built it himself, even cutting the silk for the gas-bag over a pattern that Mr. Knabenshue, the great Toledo aeronaut, cut for him. I stitched it and we both worked night and day until it was finished. Then we varnished it. We had to be very careful for if we had not watched it carefully it would have stuck together so tightly that we could not have gotten it apart, but after several days it dried sufficiently to put on another coat, and so on until we had five coats. Then we kept it inflated until the last coat was dry. Cromwell was happy then, as he could get ready to test his sky-bicycle.

Then while at one of the Columbus parks, where Cromwell was engaged to make a flight, he lost everything he had by fire, so all had to be done over again. He went to work and made the second outfit even better than the first, so you see what a brave little man he was. Not even a sigh, when all he had accomplished lay a heap of ashes. He turned to me and said: "Well, mother, we must commence tomorrow on our new outfit so that we can fulfill our engagements this summer."

Cromwell has always been of a mechanical nature. Having shown his preference for such things, I encouraged him, and helped him besides. He lost his father when a baby.

He attended the St. Louis balloon and air-ship carnival, where Cromwell was a great favorite and where he made a beautiful flight in his sky-cycle.

Very truly yours,
Mrs. C. Dixon

The U.S. Army's first aircraft was this dirigible, bought in 1908. But since no one could fly it except its inventor, T. S. Baldwin (near tail), it was never used.

A glum crew of young students endures the flag drill in a school pageant.

The Grownups Close In

"Penrod, what excuse have you to offer before I report your case to the principal?"
The word "principal" struck him in the vitals. Grand Inquisitor, Grand Khan, Sultan, Emperor, Tsar, Caesar Augustus—these are comparable.

PENROD, BY BOOTH TARKINGTON

The first decade was a watershed in the special world of the young. In keeping with the Victorian era just past, the decade began as a time of strict rules and frequent moralizing. At home, fathers were not inclined to spare the rod, and at the dinner table children were well scrubbed and not heard. In the classroom, whispering was an offense that merited a whipping. Sunday-school teachers darkly noted that erring mortals had once been punished with Noah's flood, and that next time God planned to finish the job with fire. In harmonious chorus, antiseptic novels and schoolbooks like the pervasive McGuffey's *Readers (pages 114-117)* sang of the rewards of virtuous behavior, warning that lazy children would come to no good end.

But as soon as the class—or dinner or chores or whipping—was over, the kids nodded their heads, promising to be good, and then raced around the corner into their own private domain. There they were self-reliant, and could fashion their own brand of happiness with nothing more than a dog or a pocketknife, or a doll and some paints. Over the course of a year, games ebbed and flowed in a mystical, unspoken sequence. Kites, for example, might be popular for a week. Then

kites would vanish and mumblety-peg or roller skates or kick-the-can or stilt-walking took over. Competition was often fierce and, in some games, the stakes were formidably high: if kids were playing "keepers" in marbles, a lost agate might set back the loser as much as 50 cents—more than a month's allowance.

But as the decade progressed, this rigid code and its underlying doctrine of self-reliance was no longer as necessary or as easy to uphold as it had been. Grownups moved in—for better or for worse—on the kids' world in ways they never had before. Daniel Beard, author of the wildly popular *American Boys Handy Book* (how to conduct snowball warfare, etc., *pages 110-113*), helped found the Boy Scouts in 1910. Publishing czar William Randolph Hearst made popular a new kind of kids' reading matter called the comic strip *(pages 102-105)*. Baseball cards, like those at right, were issued by cigarette companies in their packages as a sly bid for kids' attention. A collector's dream set would have 522 cards, but probably would not include the legendary shortstop Honus Wagner, whose picture had to be bootlegged by the tobacco companies since he refused to pose on grounds that he did not want to encourage youngsters to smoke.

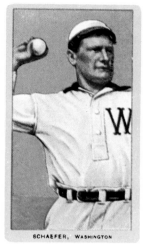

SCHAEFER, WASHINGTON

MATHEWSON, N. Y. NAT'L

CUBS

Joe Tinker OF THE CHICAGO NATIONALS

EVERS, CHICAGO NAT'L

CUBS

Frank L Chance OF THE CHICAGO NATIONALS

LAJOIE, CLEVELAND

KEELER, N. Y. AMER.

WHITE SOX

WALSH CHIC. AMER.

COBB, DETROIT

YOUNG CLEVELAND AMER.

JENNINGS, DETROIT

BENDER, PHILA. AMER.

PIRATES

OF THE PITTSBURG NATIONALS

M. BROWN, CHICAGO NAT'L

DELEHANTY, WASHINGTON

101

Spokesmen for Mischief

The Sunday funnies made a colorful entrance on the American scene on October 18, 1896, when the New York *Journal* published what it termed "eight pages of iridescent polychromous effulgence that makes the rainbow look like a lead pipe." Comic strips were an instant success and became daily features. The violent humor of the first funnies (one cartoon character performed such antics as breaking the jaw of a Negro boy and laughing merrily) was tempered to accommodate protesting parents. Pranks and embarrassing blunders be-

came staple fare in *Happy Hooligan* and *The Captain and the Kids (below and opposite),* and happy animal drawings *(top, right)* decorated the funnies page. For the first time, kids were finding something in the newspapers that reflected their own love of deviltry. When Buster Brown and his dog Tige arrived in 1902 in a strip *(overleaf)* that idealized mischief behind a thin veil of sermonizing, kids' feelings about themselves were expressed so perfectly that thousands of boys and dogs across the nation were soon sporting the names of Buster and Tige.

HAPPY HOOLIGAN

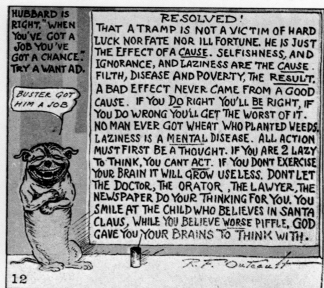

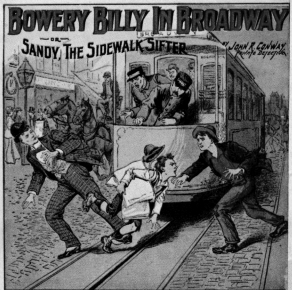

Hidden behind many a geography book full of dull facts about a country called Asia or something, there lurked a suspiciously ungeographical magazine. In the classroom, at friends' houses, almost anywhere away from the disapproving eyes of adults, boys turned to their favorite form of written fantasy, the dime novel—really a long short story bound into a five- or ten-cent magazine like those shown at left. The heroes who sprang from these pages—Fred Fearnot, Nick Carter, Bowery Billy—were personfications of the American ideal: pure of heart, doggedly ambitious and brave beyond belief.

The greatest of all dime-novel heroes was Frank Merriwell *(pages 108-109)*, created for *Tip Top Weekly* by George Patten, alias Burt L. Standish. Patten wrote some 20,000 words a week and reached 125 million readers, but virtue had to be its own reward, for he received a maximum of $150 per issue, and died in poverty.

His fictional creation had a far better time of it. Frank Merriwell, in fact, could do no wrong. As Patten wrote, "His handsome proportions, his graceful, muscular figure, his fine, kingly head and that look of clean manliness . . . stamped him as a fellow of lofty thoughts and ambitions." First at Fardale Academy, then at Yale College, and later during world-wide adventures, the magnetic Frank Merriwell accomplished every task with perfect ease. Time and time again, he won the day in boxing, baseball (he possessed a pitch that curved in two directions), football, hockey, lacrosse, crew, track, shooting, bicycle racing, billiards and golf. He outwitted Chinese bandits, Texas rustlers and urban thugs. In addition to his feats of brain and muscle, he was *good*. When classmates stole a turkey from a farmer as a prank, Frank stayed behind to pin a five-dollar bill to the roost. He loved his mother, his alma mater and his country; he abhorred poor sportsmanship, drinking and bullies. The creator of this paragon of virtue once said, "I confess that my imagination was often pumped pretty dry," but for 20 years, he turned out such thrilling episodes as the one on the following pages.

Jack Presley was the first to understand the girl's danger. Darting forward, he sprang right in front of the rushing horses, caught her up in his arms and staggered out of harm's way.

Tip Top Weekly

An ideal publication ··· for the American Youth

Issued Weekly. By Subscription $2.50 per year. Entered as Second Class Matter at New York Post Office by STREET & SMITH, 238 William St., N. Y.

No. 269.   **Price, Five Cents.**

Frank Merriwell's Great Victory
or The Effort of His Life

BY
BURT L. STANDISH

FRANK LITERALLY FLUNG HIMSELF FORWARD WITH A LAST GREAT BURST OF SPEED, BREASTED THE TAPE, AND PLUNGED INTO THE ARMS OF BART HODGE.

An Average Day for Frank

During one spring season Frank Merriwell was so busy starring on the baseball team and bidding for top place in his Yale class that he had no time for track. So he trained his friend Bart Hodge to run against Hood of Harvard in the mile event of the intercollegiate track meet. Unfortunately, Bart sprained his ankle at the very last moment, but he decided to run anyway.

Preparations were being made for the mile run. Bart joined the starters. Then, at the last moment before the men were called to the mark, a great mad roar went up from the Yale stand. "Merriwell! Merriwell! Merriwell!"

Frank Merriwell was seen running across the field. "On your mark!" cried the starter. The men leaned forward on the line. "Set!" There was a straining of muscles. The runners crouched like human wolves ready for the spring.

Bang! Away they went. Frank Merriwell had reached the field in time to take his place as the substitute of Bart Hodge. He shot off from the mark with Dalton of Columbia at his shoulder.

Merriwell had counted on taking his pace from Hood, and he was disappointed when the man permitted Fealing of Georgetown and Dalton of Columbia to draw away. His disappointment increased as still others took the lead.

It occurred to him that Hood was playing a crafty trick. He was willing to sacrifice himself in order that Harvard might come out ahead of Yale. In order for Yale to take the lead she must win this event, while Harvard could lose it and still be at the top by a small margin.

At the half Frank gradually increased his speed. Old coaches looked on in consternation as they saw Frank pass man after man in that quarter. It seemed that he had made his burst too soon.

Now Merriwell felt the terrible strain, and he realized that Hood had used him to set the pace.

"Tricked!" groaned a Yale coach. "Merriwell can't keep it up to the tape!"

Now Hood was pressing Frank, who began to feel that he could not carry out the mighty task, yet who would not give his body the least relaxing. Every muscle of that splendid frame was tense, every nerve was strained. Frank's face was white as chalk. Once he seemed to reel. In that moment Hood reached his side and took the lead by twenty-six inches.

A cloudlike mist fluttered before Frank Merriwell's eyes. He knew that Hood had passed him. Through the cloud he saw grotesquely dancing figures beyond the finish. But his ears were deaf from the wild yells of the thousands.

"Come on, Merriwell—come on!"

"Hood wins!" roared the Crimson. "Har-vard! Har-vard!"

Frank knew the finish must be near. He gathered himself for the effort of his life. Then, just when it seemed that defeat was certain, he literally flung himself forward with a last burst of speed, passed the side of the Harvard runner, breasted the tape and plunged into the arms of Bart Hodge.

He had dropped, and like a mighty Niagara rose the roar that greeted the victor, for Merriwell had won at the last moment, and Yale was in the lead.

Roar! Roar! Roar! It went up to the blue sky! Men hugged each other, pounded each other, shrieked, danced and also died with joy.

"Merriwell!" roared the throng. "Merriwell! Merriwell!"

Set among mementos of the era, the "Handy Books" by Dan Beard and his sisters were among the most prized possessions of kids who devised their own playthings.

Guidebooks to the Kids' World

"I'd rather be an American boy than President of the United States, or anything else in the world," Daniel Carter Beard once said. In 1882, Beard—who, as a young man, worked at various times as an illustrator, engineer and map maker—magnificently regressed to childhood and wrote a compendium of kids' lore, *The American Boys Handy Book*. No sugary dose of adult wistfulness, the *Handy Book* described in simple terms how to build kites, snowshoes or sailboats, how to stuff birds, trap rabbits or raise frogs. Beard's sisters later wrote a similar, though less mechanical, guide for girls. For generations of youngsters, these volumes, excerpted below with illustrations on the following pages, were indispensable reference works on the real art of growing up.

HOW TO MAKE AN ARMED WAR KITE

These aero-nautical cutters might be appropriately named the Scorpion, "Stingerree," Wasp, or Hornet, because they fight with their tails. To win the battle you so manoeuvre your warrior that its tail sweeps across and cuts the string of your antagonist. The cutters to be attached to the tail are made of sharp pieces of broken glass called knives. Fasten three knives together with wax so that each shall point in a different direction, bind on this three slips of thin wood lengthwise to hold the wax and glass firmly, and cover neatly with cloth or kid. Boys participating in this war of kites should always bear in mind the fact that it requires but little skill to cut an unarmed kite, and that there is no honor or glory to be gained in vanquishing a foe who is unable to defend himself.

HOW TO MAKE A BOOMERANG

With boiling water scald a piece of well-seasoned elm, ash or hickory plank that is free from knots. Allow the wood to remain in water until it becomes pliable enough to bend. When it has assumed the proper curve, nail on the side pieces to hold the wood in position until it is thoroughly dry; after which the side pieces may be removed, with no fear that the plank will not retain the curve imparted. Saw the wood into as many pieces as it will allow, and each piece will be a boomerang that only needs to be trimmed with a pocket knife, and scraped smooth with a piece of glass to make a finished weapon. A boomerang cast by a beginner is very dangerous

in a crowd, for there is no telling where it is going to alight, and when it does come down it sometimes comes with a force enough to cut a small dog almost in two.

TAXIDERMY—HOW TO SKIN A BIRD

Place the bird on its back upon the table, in such a position that the head will be toward your left hand; then, with the knife in your right hand you are ready to make the incision. With your left hand separate the feathers, left and right, from the apex of the breast bone to the tail. Cut a straight slit through the skin between these points. . . .

HOW TO ORGANIZE A GIRLS' CLUB

Make out a list of the girls you intend to invite to join the club, and ask them to meet at your house. Explain your plans, and let the would-be members sign the constitution, which should previously be neatly written out in a blank book, with the name of the club, date, and the full name of the founder of the society. Later, if the club finds the constitution adopted inadequate for its needs, it may be amended to suit the society.

MAINTAINING YOUR BICYCLE

The arrangement of the holes for oiling of bicycles varies with each make; but, bear in mind, wherever there is friction, oil is needed, and if you examine your wheel carefully you will find that this has been provided for. Look for oiling points on front and rear axles, crank-axle bearings, pedals, steering head, brake-lever, brake-spoon, chain at joints if oil is used on chain.

Sticks plus snow make a snowman

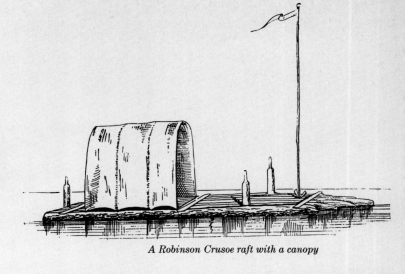

A Robinson Crusoe raft with a canopy

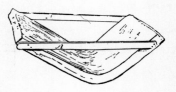

Three stages in the making of a boomerang

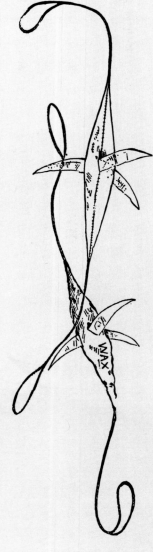

Tails for an armed war kite

Knots for every need

Listening to a telephone . . .

Lore of the Handy Books

In the true spirit of childhood, the creations of the *Handy Books* achieved a maximum of happiness with a minimum of materials. Telephones *(far left and far right)* were made of baking-powder boxes, drawing paper and string; a raft was made of logs fastened together with wooden pegs ("they will hold much more firmly than iron nails," wrote Dan Beard). The cheapest and most important ingredient of all was imagination—the kids' own.

A daisy fan made with paper

A moving head
in a Christmas card

The Christmas card complete

A mirror to fool an audience for a play

A doll made
out of a corn husk

A beeswax candle
in a walnut boat

A straw hat tied into
shape for a workbasket

Drying out flowers in sand

. . . and speaking into the telephone

113

Dear Old Golden Rule Days

School, that unavoidable misfortune which befell all freedom-loving kids, offered a rather somber introduction to the world of books. While in some urban schools children were beginning to learn by doing things themselves *(right)*, millions of youngsters still cut their reading teeth on a five-book series known as McGuffey's *Readers*, containing short tales *(below)*, verses, pronunciation and spelling lessons, and an anthology of English and American literature. Written in the 1830s and 1840s by a university professor named William Holmes McGuffey, they remained the literary staple for countless schools well into the 20th Century. McGuffey grew up on a farm chopped out of the Ohio wilderness, and his *Readers* were successful because in an America still predominantly rural they spoke the language of rural children.

Charles was an honest boy, but his neighbor, Jack Pilfer, was a thief. Charles would not take anything which did not belong to him; but Jack would take whatever he could get.

Early one summer's morning, as Charles was going to school, he met a man who had oranges to sell. The man wished to stop and get his breakfast, and asked Charles if he would hold his horse while he went into the house.

But he first inquired of the landlord if he knew Charles to be an honest boy, as he would not like to trust his oranges with him, if he was not.

Yes, said the landlord, I have known Charles all his life, and have never known him to lie or steal; all the neighbors know him to be an honest boy, and I will engage your oranges will be as safe with him as with yourself.

The orange man then put the bridle into Charles' hand, and went into the house to eat his breakfast.

Very soon Jack Pilfer came along the road and seeing Charles holding the horse, he asked him whose horse he had

The Eskimo
makes his house
of snow blocks.
He has no wood
in his cold country.
Can a snow house
keep him warm?

Youthful investigators, urged on by a rather heavy-handed message from the blackboard, tackle the Eskimo Housing Question during a 1904 geography lesson.

there, and what was in the baskets. Charles told him that the owner of the horse was in the house, and that there were oranges in the baskets.

As soon as Jack found there were oranges in the baskets, he determined to have one, and going up to the basket, he slipped in his hand and took out one of the largest, and was making off with it.

But Charles said, Jack, you shall not steal these oranges while I have the care of them, and so you may just put that one back into the basket.

Not I, said Jack, as I am the largest, I shall do as I please; but Charles was not afraid, and taking the orange out of his hand, he threw it back into the basket.

Jack then attempted to go around to the other side and take one from the other basket; but as he stepped too near the horse's heels, he received a violent kick, which sent him sprawling to the ground.

His cries soon brought out the people from the house, and when they learned what had happened, they said that Jack was rightly served; and the orange man, taking Charles' hat, filled it with oranges, as he said he had been so faithful in guarding them, he should have all these for honesty.

QUESTIONS

1. What is this story about?
2. Which is the honest boy?
3. What kind of boy was Jack Pilfer?
4. What is the job of a landlord?
5. What kind of character did the landlord give Charles?
6. How can boys secure a good name?
7. What advantage is there in possessing a good character?

A botany lesson, aided by a lavish display of flowers imported into the classroom, elicits rapt attention from tiny grammar-school children in Washington, D.C.

An oddly assorted but dutiful public-school orchestra, with a barefoot cello player in the front row, tunes up at the first schoolhouse in St. Petersburg, Florida.

Freed for the day by the final school bell, boys and girls clamber up ladders and through the pipework of an ingenious early playground structure in Denver.

The Old Hometown

Main Street in Dorrance, Kansas, seen from the town's water tower, snakes off into prairie.

Life in a Prairie Town

This town is the fruit of great aspiration, and we who live here now have a debt to posterity that we can pay only by still achieving, still pursuing; we must learn to labor and to wait.

WILLIAM ALLEN WHITE, EDITOR OF THE EMPORIA, KANSAS, *GAZETTE*

Patience was a way of life for at least 45 million Americans at the turn of the century. Those millions, comprising the 60 per cent of the population that resided in towns of fewer than 2,500 people, endured as country folk always had, in the grip of the seasons, following the rhythm of planting and harvesting. So it was for the wheatgrowers of Dorrance, an austere little town huddled on a windy prairie in north-central Kansas.

During its half-century of existence, Dorrance had never been more than a speck on the map, but it had seen a lot of history. The area had been crossed by Indian hunters, by wagon trains of settlers and gold seekers. In 1867, the Union Pacific Railroad tracks reached Dorrance, bringing with them the German, Irish and other immigrants who accounted for much of the town's modest growth after 1870. By 1910, when Dorrance was incorporated, it had only 281 citizens, yet it was one of the most important towns in Russell County.

Not without cause, the townspeople took quiet pride in their community. Dorrance had everything a country town really needed: a good public school, with four teachers and about 100 pupils; a bank and a hotel; four churches; a variety of stores and businesses; telephone and telegraph service. This was a progressive town. Decades ago, farmers had built windmills that still pumped their water. Recently a few men had acquired modern steam-driven threshers, and the Mahoney family even bought a car when autos were still a novelty in the cities.

The people themselves, shown here in pictures taken by Leslie Halbe, the banker's son, were exactly what their town suggested: a plain, durable folk who feared God and worked hard. In their need for relief from the prairie's raw isolation, people drew together and got on well. German and Frenchman, Catholic and Mennonite pitched in to help one another at harvest time, and to outfit the town's baseball team. No one got rich, but no one was poor.

In such small towns life had a continuity that extended beyond the grave. The dead, buried in cemeteries inside the town, were as much a part of Dorrance as the blacksmith's shop and Weber's lumberyard; their graves were visited on Decoration Day by all the citizens, led by Civil War veterans in faded uniforms. Few people, living or dead, left Dorrance; almost everyone stayed on, content and patient to labor and to wait.

Dorrance's station crew waits for a train under a sign listing distances to the nearest big cities. Here salesmen detrained and hawked their wares for miles around.

Two landmarks on Main Street, the post office and village drugstore, were built of limestone from nearby quarries and lumber that had to be brought in by rail.

Dorrance's telephone switchboard operator had few calls and plenty of time to chat. Twice, she had no work at all when blizzards knocked down all the wires.

The Citizens' State Bank issued loans to families between harvests. One major cause for seasonal borrowing was the average farmer's need for a dozen work horses.

Under hats pegged to the wall, town workers and visitors on business are served family style by a dexterous short-order cook in Sheetz's Restaurant on Main Street.

Wearing their Sunday suits and straw boaters, two young farmers, Peter Steinle and Henry Heinze, share a buggy ride to Dorrance from their outlying spread.

The Lutheran Church lets out its congregation, about 60 families strong. Dorrance had three other denominations, all with white frame churches of their own.

A wheatgrower unloads his crop at a grain elevator. This elevator was constructed by German immigrants who brought with them the winter wheat grown locally.

A farmer sets out from the local John Deere dealership with a new header machine to reap his wheat. Harvesting began around July 1 and took about 12 days.

A man identified as S. Shilts tended pigs to supplement the income from his wheat crop. A typical Dorrance farmer, he cultivated about 300 acres of prairie land.

Helping at harvest time, a wheat farmer's family gathers together on the water wagon driven out to refill the steam engine that powered the threshing machine.

Big City Down River

One hundred miles to the east of Dorrance lay the bigger, more bumptious hometown of Junction City, Kansas. Thanks to its handy location at the junction of the Republican and Smoky Hill Rivers, it was a thriving business center of 5,000 citizens. And there was not one of them who was not proud of the way the town had grown: by 1900 there were a full score of restaurants. The matching complement of drug, department and food stores drew the farmers from miles around and kept the natives prosperous. At right and on the following pages is a sampling of these Junction City emporiums, together with lists of prices a shopper in the town—and thousands of other towns much like it—paid in the first decade.

Drugstore Prices

SODA FOUNTAIN

Ice Cream Soda	10¢	Grape Lemonade	15¢
Plain Soda	5¢	Orangeade	5¢
Root Beer Float	5¢	Lemon Phosphate	5¢
Sundae	10¢	Buttermilk	5¢
Cantaloupe Sundae	15¢	Egg Milk Chocolate	10¢
Egg Drinks	10¢	Coffee (iced or hot)	10¢
Tonic Water	10¢	Cakes	5¢

DRUGS

Witch Hazel	25¢	Corn Plasters	10¢
Aruica Salve	10¢	Wart Remover	10¢
Bromo Seltzer	10¢	Castoria	35¢
Wine of Cardui	$1.00	St. Jacob's Oil	25¢
Cough Syrup	25¢	Hair Balsam	50¢

The Loeb & Hollis Drug Store, one of the best in Junction City, sold perfume, cigars and "fancy goods," and had a soda fountain, latest in drugstore fixtures.

Frey's New Cafe, on the main street, was open all night, and served such delicacies as oysters in season. The stairs (upper left) led to private dining rooms.

Dinner Menu

APPETIZERS

Canteloupe, half	10¢	Sliced Tomatoes	10¢
Sliced Orange	10¢	New Radishes	5¢
Young Onions	5¢	Sliced Cucumbers	10¢

SOUP
Old Fashioned Navy Bean, 10¢

MAIN COURSE

Channel Catfish	20¢	Chicken Fricassee	20¢
Pork Tenderloins	20¢	Roast Beef	15¢
Omelet with Jelly	15¢	Pork and Beans	15¢
Roast Pork, Apple Sauce	20¢	Boston Baked Beans	10¢

VEGETABLES

Corn on the Cob	10¢	Pickled Beets	5¢
Buttered Beets	5¢	Cold Slaw	5¢
Mashed Potatoes	5¢	Salad	10¢

DESSERT

Lemon Layer Cake	5¢	Raspberries and Cream	10¢
Ice Cream	10¢	Rhubarb Pie	5¢
Ice Cream and Cake	15¢	Green Apple Pie	5¢

BEVERAGES

Coffee	5¢	Tea	5¢
Milk	5¢	Buttermilk	5¢

Aproned butchers at the Park Meat Market, named for its parkside location, stand ready to cut a customer's meats to order. Wild game was a shop specialty.

Meat and Poultry Prices

Spring Chicken	7¢ lb.	Roosters	15¢ ea.	Turkey	10¢ lb.	Veal	10¢ lb.
Beef	10¢ lb.	Hens	7¢ lb.	Duck	6¢ lb.	Breakfast Bacon	12½¢ lb.
Sausage	12½¢ lb.	Pork	10¢ lb.	Duck, Dressed	10¢ lb.	Goose	5¢ lb.

Grocery Prices

PRODUCE AND DAIRY PRODUCTS

Red Apples	30¢ pk.	Dried Apricots	10¢ lb.
Seed Potatoes	35¢ bu.	Dried Prunes	5¢ lb.
Onion Sets	3 qt. 25¢	Eggs	12¢ doz.
Oranges	20¢ doz.	Butter	18¢ lb.
Lemons	15¢ doz.	Swiss Cheese	25¢ lb.

HOUSEWARES

Scrub Brush	15¢	Starch	10¢
Lye	5¢	Toilet Soap	3 for 15¢
Garden Seed	2 for 5¢	Candles	1 Box 15¢

CANNED GOODS

Golden Cream Corn	10¢	Boston Baked Beans	10¢
String Beans	10¢	Oysters	20¢
Tomatoes	20¢	Jams	10¢
Early June Peas	10¢	Green Turtle Meat	$2.75
Sliced Peaches	25¢	Sardines in Oil	5¢

STAPLES

Tea	40¢	Sugar	100 lbs. $5.80
Coffee	15¢ lb.	Salt	100 lbs. 20¢
Cocoa	25¢	Salad Dressing	25¢
Macaroni	10¢	Baking Powder	10¢
Hominy Grits	10¢	Gelatine	15¢

Latham's Grocery had staples (in bins, left), canned goods and produce. The wood stove, which provided the store's only heat, and a coffee mill stand at the rear.

Department Store Prices

LADIES' WEAR

Tailor-made Suit	$10.00	Waist	$3.00
Skirt	$4.00	Corset	40¢
Chemise	50¢	Shawl	50¢
Bracelet	35¢	Silk Petticoat	$5.00
Shoes	$1.50	Bead Purse	59¢

MEN'S WEAR

Fancy Suit	$9.00	Coat and Vest	$7.00
Trousers	$1.25	Linen Collar	25¢
Shirts	50¢	Hat	$2.00
Woolen hose	15¢	Underwear	50¢
Suspenders	25¢	Work Shoes	$1.25

HOUSE FURNISHINGS

Blanket	35¢	Wallpaper	roll 5¢
Carpet	12¢ yd.	42-Piece Dinner Set	$2.95
Hammock	$3.50	Sheet, Double Bed	58¢

DRESS GOODS

Gingham	12½¢ yd.	Sewing Machine	$12.00
Madras Cloth	10¢ yd.	Embroidery	8¢
Taffeta	85¢ yd.	Silk	50¢ yd.
Calico	6¢ yd.	Sewing Pattern	10¢
Pins	box 5¢	Damask	40¢ yd

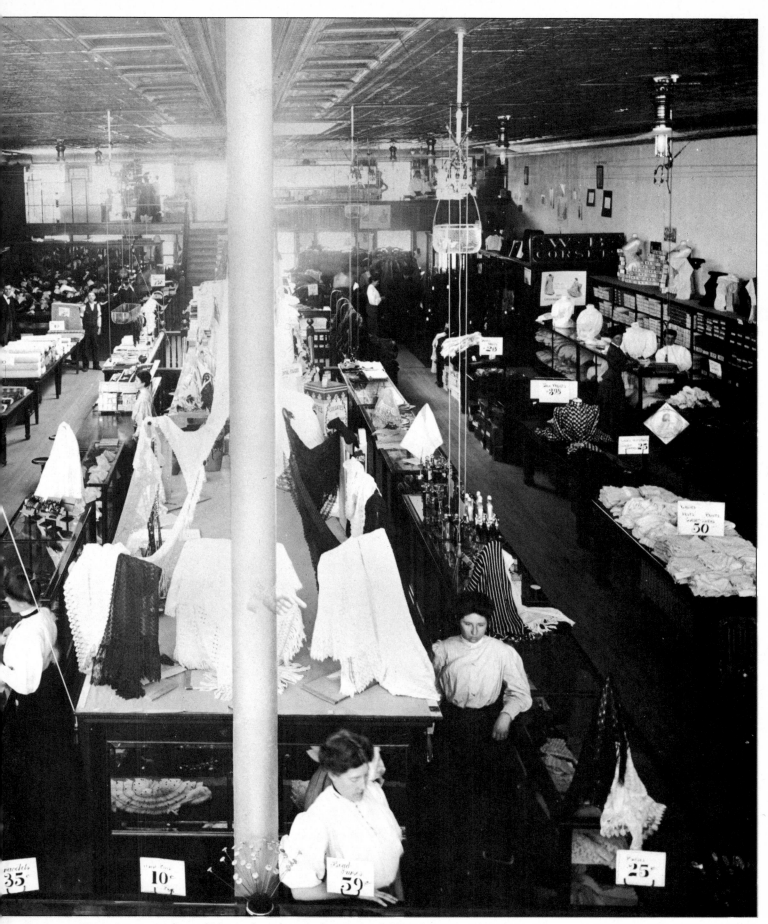

The Pegues, Wright Department Store sold dry goods on the main floor. Baskets holding the customers' change and receipts clacked to and fro on overhead trolleys.

An American Family Album

Us on the porch

In 1900 the hometown folks had a new toy to play with—the Kodak Brownie camera, which suddenly made its appearance at the modest price of one dollar. All a person had to do was snap the shutter, and there were Mama, Papa and the kids—at home, on vacation or in school—in stiff but familiar poses that were pasted in photo albums all over America.

The pictures on these pages were made by just such amateur portraitists. The snapshot above is of the Shaw family of Eau Claire, Wisconsin. The widow of George Shaw, a lumber baron, sits at the left in

the back. Next to her is her son George Jr., then in high school; to the right stands his aunt, Mrs. Eugene Shaw. Margaret Shaw, Eugene's daughter, sits in front; the boy beside her and the young lady behind him are family friends.

The pictures at right and on the following pages were taken by kindred amateurs. Resurrected from dusty attics and library shelves—some with the subjects' names long forgotten but many with the original captions intact—they make up a homely portrait of the early years of the century.

Sunday afternoon

Here we are in a lumberyard

Making Thanksgiving pies

At Uncle Herman's house

The Campbells are coming

The Campbells are going

Fishing for a compliment

Four on a melon

The big play

Vacation Frolics

Summer was a time for outdoor frolics, and for just lazing around. The whole family might go to a shore resort, like the Campbells of Michigan *(upper right, on buoy, and opposite page)*, or to a camp in the woods, like the Wooldridges of Arizona *(above)*. A daughter home from school might treat her classmates to a fortnight's house party, like Esther Eva Strauss, who is eating watermelon with a cluster of school chums *(left)*.

House-party entertainment, like summer capers generally, was homemade. The girls' gentlemen callers would come from miles around, riding horseback or driving their fanciest rigs—buggies and phaetons. They amused themselves at tennis on the lawn, hayrides on wagons, teas by the riverbank or deep in the woods; at chestnut-roasting and marshmallow-toasting; at fishing from a pier, like the hatted girl on the opposite page. Wherever they went and however they passed the time, the Brownie camera went along to chronicle the fun.

Speaking of buoys

Making merry on the Chippewa

Four little maids from school are we

Whew—passed calculus

Off to College

For understandable reasons, family albums had a notable shortage of pictures of students laboring over their books—drudgery being a highly unmemorable experience. But the antics and comradeship of college days received plenty of attention. Who could forget the day when the girls at Beloit College gave a party in the dormitory, or the time they poked their heads through a sheet *(top right)* to pose as Bluebeard's hapless wives? And remember the night after

You'll never take us alive!

Life is a cinch

Bluebeard's wives

final exams *(right)*—or even the morning after the night before *(left)*—when the awful threat of the dean's ax had finally been erased? These and other pieces of nostalgic trivia found their way into family picture collections, to be pulled out years later and chuckled over by the subjects, or roundly hooted at by irreverent spouses. And the children, while wondering how their parents could act so undignified, decided that maybe the old folks had not been so hopelessly stodgy after all.

The passing of exams—in March's room

The hungry bunch

Gate swingers

It's all bluff

"Catch anything, Miss?"

All aboard

Why the old gray mare is tired

Looks comfy

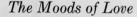

The Moods of Love

The box Brownie was a sensitive recorder of small moments to be remembered. Perhaps because the person who took the picture usually was a friend or a relative, courting couples found it easy to share the spirit of the moment with the camera. And those were moments that could not be allowed to fade, unrecorded, into the past. There was Horace Rhoads on a California pier *(far left)*, holding a parasol for the girl who became his wife. There, in a goofy hat *(above left)*, was a Midwestern Romeo grinning at a friend; and four youngsters *(left)* sitting in mock formality in another hammock. Clowning, flirting, chatting or kissing, lovers in all the little moods of courtship were shown in the family album.

Underneath the bough

A girls' basketball squad, evidence of the more active life women found in the new century, poses for the team picture.

The Ladies

A Woman's Place

In other countries you may be gently urged for an appreciation of the architecture of galleries; but the American man will, in nine cases out of ten, make his first question of the visiting foreigner—"Well, what do you think of our women?"

KATHERINE G. BUSBEY, 1910

When George Bernard Shaw was asked his opinion of American women in 1907, he answered: "Every American woman explains that she is an absolute exception and is not like any other American woman. But they are all exactly the same. The only thing to be said for them is they are usually very well dressed and extraordinarily good looking." That was exactly the way American men wanted their women: beautiful, but not so bright and sassy that they wandered from their place in the home.

The emancipation of women from male domination—as well as from fanciful costumes requiring steel-reinforced corsets (*right*) and a life close to the hearth—was barely beginning as the century dawned. Fully one quarter of the states then in the Union denied a wife the right to own property; one third of them allowed her no claim on her own earnings—even if she worked to support a shiftless husband. And 36 of them, or four fifths, denied her an equal share in the guardianship of her children.

Peons the women may have seemed, but powerless they were not. Despite their lack of legal rights, they had many a compensation. "They haven't th' right to vote," conceded Mr. Dooley, the fictitious philosopher created by humorist Finley Peter Dunne, "but they have th' priv'lege iv controllin' th' man ye ilicit. They haven't th' right to make laws, but they have th' priv'lege iv breakin' thim, which is betther. They haven't the right iv a fair thrile be a jury iv their peers; but they have th' priv'lege iv an unfair thrile be a jury iv their admirin' infeeryors. If I cud fly d'ye think I'd want to walk?"

Most women, as Mr. Dooley suggested, chose to "fly." They got their way exactly as they were expected to, by dazzling their menfolk with feminine wiles. In this course they were abetted by a flood of "women's literature"—romantic fiction that created an ideal of the softly genteel but indomitable female, and magazines that gave them practical how-to instructions for achieving the ideal. Articles preached decorum and cautioned against dangerous new ideas. *Vogue* warned in 1900, "All decent people are agreed that the emancipated novelists are not fit reading," and listed as taboo the "cancerous literature" of Ibsen, Zola and Shaw among others. Along with such admonitions went a steady stream of advice on beauty and fashion, which, as the acid Shaw noted, was American woman's most obvious asset.